CAKE THERAPY:

HOW BAKING CHANGED MY LIFE

ALTREISHA N. FOSTER

Copyright © 2023 by Altreisha N. Foster

All rights reserved. No part of this publication may be reproduced, distributed, or transmitted in any form or by any means, including photocopying, recording, or other electronic or mechanical methods, without the prior written permission of the publisher, except in the case of brief quotations embodied in critical reviews and certain other noncommercial uses permitted by copyright law.

Cover Photo: Dotun Ayodeji (The Light Source Company)

Cover Design: Kristoffe Lawrence

Book Design by HMDpublishing

*To my mom, Lorna, and my brother, Nickoy,
my anchors*

FOREWORD

One of the many amazing benefits of my job as a Lifestyle Editor has been interactions with individuals like Dr. Altreisha Foster.

Hers was a feature I'd happened upon in *People* magazine. The Jamaican-born Minnesota pastry chef created the celebratory cake for the 200th episode of *The Bachelor* spin-off, *The Bachelorette*. Little did I know that I'd merely scratched the surface and that we'd develop a strong bond!

Altreisha's story, as told here, will stir the imagination of many. Her journey is one of triumph against all odds, of healing, and of lifting others—girls, especially.

The pages are sprinkled with love via personal recipes. Creating spectacular desserts requires time, patience, and lots of love. This is what has contributed to the healing she is now experiencing.

"Cake Therapy," she shared with me, "has also saved me. It has snatched me from the jaws of post-partum depression and has become my center."

Altreisha is a proud Jamaican, deathly shy, humble and uber-private. She is a mother, a wife. She is Lorna's daughter, Maas Tiny and Miss Girly's granddaughter. A woman born from poverty, a broken home, broken lives, a survivor of adult indiscretions, but she bakes through the pain, the memories of past hurt.

She is alive, she is here... here for us.

When I think of Altreisha, I think of the words of architect R Buckminster Fuller: "The purpose of our lives is to add value to the people of this generation and those that follow."

Novia McDonald-Whyte
Editor, Lifestyle & Social Content
The Jamaica Observer

CONTENTS

Preface	ix
Introduction	1
Let Me Introduce Myself	5
Growing up in Golden River	11
Mom	21
The Man Who Fathered Me	33
Family	45
Leaving Golden River	59
Spanish Town	65
Education in Jamaica	69
The McLeods	83
Leaving Jamaica	89
The Rossers	97
Howard University	103
Friendships	109
Trauma	121
Professional Life	137
Marriage and children	141
Baking	149
Reflections	165
Afterword	175
Acknowledgments	179

PREFACE

My inspiration for writing this book came out of the blue, as it were. Up until the time when inspiration hit, I'd had no intention of writing anything, except academic papers and probably a few recipes. However, after doing an interview with the *Jamaica Observer*, one of the daily newspapers in Jamaica, and a subsequent interview with Simone Clarke-Cooper of local station *Television Jamaica (TVJ)*, I thought *Wow, cake has brought me to this place, and people are noticing me and learning about me. Probably it's time to reveal who I am!*

But that idea was more easily conceived than the act of putting it into action. Even when I was on the television, I felt like I was still hiding myself, and I thought Simone saw right through me, because during our conversation she said, "You seem to have a story, Doc. I see a book in your future."

Instinctively, I immediately dismissed the idea of writing a book about myself. Even though I thought that it was time to reveal myself to the world, I balked at actually doing it. That was my defense mechanism kicking into action. If I wrote a book, I'd have to share myself with the world—I'd have to reveal myself, and by force of habit, I wanted to keep on hiding—to repress the pain. I wanted to keep the unpleasantness of my past hidden.

However, Simone's comments caused me to stop and think about my life. I mentor girls. I encourage them to be themselves—to share their opinions, and to seek help when they need it. But at the same time, I wasn't sharing myself. I wasn't sharing my story with them.

I was hiding.

When I mentor girls, I don't tell them about my struggles. I relate to them from a standpoint of once being poor and rising above poverty. I do not share some of the things that made me who I am today, some of the things that crippled me and held me hostage for a long time.

It was in that moment that I realized I needed to share myself with these girls. I needed to let them into the secrets of my life and show them how I've been dealing with them. I want to let them know that, while there are all kinds of obstacles along life's way, they can overcome them just as I have done. They simply need to have grit and determination and the spirit of perseverance, no matter what they are going through.

In writing this book, I also wanted to share myself finally with my friends and colleagues. I wanted to free myself of the story of how I came to be who I am today, with the hope that I would gain some catharsis.

And I have.

I hope that girls and women living in Jamaica particularly, and girls and women who live outside of Jamaica, who share a similar story to mine—a missing dad, a single mother, facing trauma—can hear my voice and know that there is indeed hope after they have struggled through the darkest of tunnels. I want them to know that if they believe in themselves and work toward achieving their dreams, the possibilities for them are endless.

Moreover, I want to let go of the stories that I've kept secret all this time, so that I can move on to the next chapter in the book that my life is shaping up to be.

This book is my apology tour, of sorts, for the friends who chose me and have waited to meet the real me. It is also my apology tour for all the other people in my life: family, relatives, colleagues, and acquaintances. Upon reading, they will get to know me—well, most of me, because I'm still a work in progress. I'm still working through the issues that I hope to put to rest sooner than later.

Dr. Altreisha Nass-sheva Foster
February 2023

INTRODUCTION

This book sets about accomplishing several things.

First, it tells the story of how the traumas that have dogged my footsteps for a long time caused me to hide the real me from everyone who has walked in and out of my life, as well as those who have stayed, and how I am now learning to reveal myself to them. Second, it tells the story of how my brokenness, caused by a life of social and economic hardships which traumatized me, is being healed, after I discovered my gift of baking. Third, it reveals my new mindset as I step into my purpose.

This book is aimed at women and girls in difficult situations—being impoverished and not being able to make ends meet, being abused, being constantly judged, lacking confidence, confused, feeling as if you don't fit in and wondering if you will ever achieve your dreams and change your circumstances. You should know that you can nurture your dreams and believe that it is possible to realize them. Yours should be a belief in the possible.

Belief, with hard work and a bit of luck, is the key to releasing your dreams in a tangible way. You don't know in which direction your luck lies, but that it *is* there. You have to start taking the necessary steps toward your dream, and that luck will reveal itself.

Know that your situation does not define who you are and who you can actually become. The obstacles that are placed in your way are ultimately steppingstones, because you have to step on them and walk from one to the other, making sure you keep your balance.

Know that even the person who is broken, the person who is talked about most despicably and the person who is suffering innumerable hurts can survive and become somebody. But you have to believe that you have the power and the potential to change your circumstances. I had the potential to change my circumstances, and I've exploited that potential. You can do that, too. But you have to have a strong belief that you can.

If you don't have a strong belief in your capabilities to achieve your life's goal, you will be forever stuck in your current situation. You may have a dream, but without belief that you can achieve it, you aren't going anywhere. Belief is the thing that will cause you to put in all the effort to make the dream that you have of your life a reality.

At my age, I'm just now freeing myself of the baggage of my past, and finding myself. I'm finding my purpose through the work I do mentoring girls and touching their lives in a positive way. You, like everyone else, have a purpose. The key to finding your purpose is self-belief. I am living proof of what belief in the self can do. However, sometimes you need a guardian angel to help you find it. Believe me, I know. Guardian angels have been invaluable in helping me achieve my success.

There are eighteen chapters in this book—I know, eighteen! These chapters hold the stories of my life that I'm finally sharing with you. Each chapter tells one aspect of my story. The stories that you'll read in each chapter overlap, and at the end of the book, you should be able to put the pieces of the puzzle of my life together. What you will find after you've done that is me—Dr. Altreisha Nass-Sheva Foster.

Note that each chapter starts with a recipe for a dessert. These desserts remind me of particular experiences I've had, good and bad, and even experiences I wish I'd had. These recipes represent how food has helped me to peel back the onion that is my life, one layer at a time—retrospectively.

You are about to read:

- How, for most of my life, I've kept parts of me hidden from everyone and the reasons why I chose to hide myself.

- How baking allowed me to explore, thrive, and be seen, but how I still strive, even now, to remain hidden to maintain some privacy.

- How I gained the confidence to remove most of the veil that I have been hiding behind for most of my life.

- How I'm ready to step into my purpose by paying it forward after winning my battles.

I wish I could have been more transparent about the issues with which I was grappling for much of my life with my family, my friends and acquaintances, but those issues caused me to close off a part of me from the world—the world being my family, friends and people I've met along the journey of my life. I'm rectifying this omission with this book.

I hope that you find some insight about your own life and the lives of the people close to you after reading the book, and that it will give you some hope and strengthen your resolve to keep on moving toward where you want to be.

CHAPTER 1
LET ME INTRODUCE MYSELF

PAVLOVA BITES WITH PRALINE SAUCE

This deconstructed dessert represents my metamorphosis. It is novel and innovative, and it represents my mindset to never settle for the ordinary and to never settle for the status quo. It represents my evolution and my ability to adapt, to shift and be able to survive when situations get problematic.

Ingredients

1 ½ tsp vanilla extract (2 oz)

1/4 cup meringue powder

4 oz egg white substitute

1/2 cup water

1 1/3 cups granulated sugar

1 cup heavy whipping cream

1 cup of sugar

2 packs cream cheese

1 pack gelatin

Instructions

Preheat oven to 250°F.

In a large bowl, whip meringue powder and water with an electric mixer on high speed until soft peaks form. With the mixer running, gradually add the sugar. Whip until stiff peaks form. Add 1 tsp vanilla and whip until well combined.

Spoon the meringue into a piping bag fitted with any shaped nozzle of your liking and pipe the meringue into sizes according to your preference. Make an indentation in the center of each meringue with a tsp to form a small cup.

Place them on a baking tray lined with parchment paper.

Bake 40-45 minutes or until the outsides of meringues feel firm and crisp. Cool completely on the pan.

Whip the cream cheese, heavy cream and sugar in the mixer at medium speed until incorporated.

Add desired flavors.

Dissolve the gelatin per package direction and add 1/8 cup to the mixture, combine and chill.

Peel cooled meringue cups off the parchment paper and fill them with the chilled cream cheese mixture.

PRALINE SAUCE RECIPE

Ingredients

2 cups butter

1 cup packed brown sugar

3/4 cup coarsely chopped pecans

1 cup heavy whipping cream

1/2 tsp vanilla

Instructions

1. In a 2-quart saucepan, melt butter over medium heat. Add brown sugar and chopped pecans; cook 2 to 3 minutes, stirring frequently, until brown sugar melts and pecans smell toasted.

2. Reduce heat to low and slowly and carefully stir in whipping cream and vanilla. Return heat to medium; heat contents of pan until simmering. Cook 2 to 3 minutes, stirring constantly until thickened. Let stand 10 minutes. Drizzle sauce over Pavlova bits and serve.

Refrigerate any remaining sauce.

I've lived through four decades, and have now started on my fifth. I've met many people as I traversed this maze called life.

Some are still strangers.

Some are acquaintances.

Some are friends—very good friends at that.

But not one of them knows the real me. I have been keeping her hidden—to protect her, to keep her sane.

Mission almost accomplished!

So, it is now time for me to introduce her to myself and to you—

I have to introduce her to myself because I have been hiding her from myself for most of my life. She has been shaped by all the bad experiences that she had in her formative years. I have hidden this "me" from the world and have been showing the world a shadow of myself.

I had stacked the real me away and had refused to deal with the trauma of the past that was consuming her. But she was constantly nagging at my consciousness, urging me to put our issues into perspective.

I am listening to her now. I am about ready to take her apart and put her back together again. This time, I will be acknowledging both parts of me, and I will be actively working on treating them. I am ready to understand her. I am ready to accept her, warts and all. I have to do this before I can settle fully into my skin.

And I have to introduce her to you as well, because I want you to understand how she has been created and re-created by the trials and challenges that have pursued her through much of her life. And I want you to understand the choices she made as she endured those trials and challenges. But also, I want you to celebrate with her the victories that she has won thus far.

Four decades ago, on a sunny Saturday in June, in the community of Golden River, Above Rocks, St. Catherine, Lorna Waugh brought a beautiful baby girl into the world. That baby girl was me. She gave me the name Altreisha Nass-sheva Foster, a name unique in its own right, but one without a particular meaning, except to highlight the creativity of my mom and her younger sister.

You see, my mother and her younger sister like to make up names for the children in the family—a family tradition, I'd say. Between them, they've come up with my names, Altreisha Nass-sheva, and those of most of the children in the family.

In the family, there is a Denington, Nickoy, Lindon, Aqueleasha, Channoy, Hughmel, Uriel, Lewel, Lashana, and while I was writing this book, my niece Melanique came into this world. Even my grandmother has one of those unique names, too: Viholda. The family just has a history of making up names!

While these names may not have any special meaning, as we are told that some names have, they were all conceived out of love for the new additions to the family and to distinguish our names from the "ordinary" names that are out there—to set us apart from the pack, so to speak.

You will notice that the spelling of my name, Altreisha, does not follow the conventions of spelling words, where the letters "i" and "e" are neighbors in words. That is, the convention of putting the "i" before the "e" in such words, except when the letter "c" comes before the "i" as shown in the rule that we sang in school—"i" before "e," except after "c."

This may be seen as a mistake in the spelling of my name on the part of my mom and her younger sister. But I see it as an unconventional spelling of my name, instead of a mistake. Without knowing it at the time, they were foreshadowing the fact that not much about my life would be conventional.

As I grew older, my name took on different shapes for the people in my life—relatives, friends and acquaintances. My mother does not lose sight of my given name and what it represents to her. I, on the other hand, sometimes, introduce myself as Trisha. And when others call me Trish, I don't mind. I accept the aliases that others give me, without question, pushing my given name—the one that my mother and her younger sister labored to create—into the background, and I become what others want me to be, in that moment.

Now that I think about it, introducing myself as Trisha to some people might have been my attempt to hide my real self from the world; hiding myself has been one of my missions throughout my life. However, I have been recalibrating my mindset. Although I still respond to the aliases that friends and family choose to give me, I have no shame in shouting out my real name to the world from the rooftop.

I love this name, and I have labored to add to it. Now, I am Dr. Altreisha Nass-Sheva Foster, and this is my story.

CHAPTER 2
GROWING UP IN GOLDEN RIVER

GUAVA THUMBPRINT COOKIES

When I was growing up in Golden River, there were many guava trees, so we had lots of guavas. Some we ate straight from the tree. The rest, we made into jams and jellies. This is one recipe that we didn't make then, but it is one that I would have enjoyed. It represents the joy that comes from the little things of life. These are creamy cookies with guava jam in the middle.

Prep time: 15 mins.

Cook time: 12 mins.

Cooling time: 1 hr.

Ingredients

1 cup butter, softened

3 ounces cream cheese, softened

1 cup sugar

2 ½ cups all-purpose flour

¾ cup guava jam

1 large egg yolk room temperature

1 tbsp vanilla extract

Instructions

In the bowl of a stand mixer, cream the butter, cream cheese and sugar until light and fluffy, 5-7 minutes.

Beat in egg yolk and vanilla. Add flour and mix well. Cover and refrigerate for 1 hour or until batter is easy to handle.

Preheat oven to 350° F.

Shape dough into 1-inch balls. Place 2 inches apart on parchment-lined cookie sheets. Using the end of a wooden spoon handle or bottom of a measuring spoon, make a ½-inch-deep indentation in the center of each ball and fill each indentation with guava jam.

Bake for 10-12 minutes or until set. Remove to wire racks to cool. Then enjoy.

Life in Golden River

When I was growing up in the eighties, Golden River was your typical rural community. It was full of trees and bush, and among those trees and bush, there dwelt much life—human and non-human.

Golden River was a close-knit, family-oriented community with lots of children. My mother always told me, "It takes a village to raise a child." Well, the whole community of Golden River—relatives and non-relatives—had a hand in raising me.

Parents had no qualms about allowing their children to play together and gave them the freedom to roam around the community. There was no modern entertainment for children in the community as there is now, so our entertainment was to explore the wonders of our community, and we did this together. We were a community of children creating our own entertainment and loving it.

Generations of my family grew up in Golden River. The house in which I grew up sat on a ridge overlooking the community. That ridge is known as Pastor Ridge. The house belonged to my great-grandparents. It is the home in which my grandmother and her siblings were raised. It is the home in which my grandmother raised her children and her grandchildren. The house has eight rooms—living room, a dining room, six bedrooms and a large veranda. And it has a zinc roof on which the rain drummed on rainy days, which were many.

What remains of my family home in Pastor Ridge Jamaica.
My grandmother no longer lives here. ...
Photo Credit: Delroy Gilbert

Tons of bamboo encircled the house when I was growing up. Not much has changed since then. Through the fronds of the bamboo trees, we had glimpses of the homes and properties of family members. There was no grass in the yard when we lived there. The many kids who grew up there saw to that. Ours was the biggest yard in the community so the kids would tend to congregate there. I remember the many games that we played in that yard, barefoot: marbles, baseball, cricket and hopscotch. Those were some good times.

Generations of family members have lived on that ridge. Almost everybody who live on that ridge is a member of the family. When I was growing up, there was Brother Mike, our grandmother's uncle who lived next-door and who had a yard filled with guava trees. We did not pick those fruits, not because he stopped us from picking them but because we were afraid to go into his yard. His wife, a nice woman most times, terrified us.

Miss DinDin, whose real name I never learned, was a cousin whose property was adjacent to the right side of our yard. To get to her house, it took us not more than a few seconds to walk through the bush. We children would spend some of our days running from the yard of one relative to the next, except the yard of Brother Mike.

There were many fruit trees on the properties of our relatives, and we all enjoyed the fruits from most of those trees, without there ever being a quarrel among the relatives. Below our grandparents' house we had access to tangerines, mangoes, Otaheite apples, mangerines, ackees, bananas and lots of breadfruit.

From the front of the house, we had a good view of the family plot where generations of relatives are buried. We call that section of our property "old yard" because that was where the first house was built.

Outside, at the back of the house there was a long stairway that led from the kitchen to the main house. If we looked to the right side of the stairway, and under the cinnamon tree, we could see a chicken coop in which my grandparents reared chickens for sale. Nearby was the outhouse. Behind those buildings and through the trees, we could see the homes of other members of the family and the homes of a few members of the community who weren't family members.

The area was surrounded by plants—breadfruit trees, banana trees and tons of yam hills.

Below the cinnamon tree and down a slope, there was a jack fruit tree and a star apple tree. It is said that the star apple is the 'meanest' fruit. 'Mean' in this context being stingy. Unlike other fruits that fall when they are ripe, the star apple doesn't. It just stays on the tree until it hardens. Some people often describe others as star apples when they are not as generous as they think they should be. Still, I love star apples. I have a memory of picking some one day. I must have gotten too caught up in that task, or the star apple had refused to fall, and I was tugging at it with all my might—I'm not sure which. Before I knew what was happening, I was rolling down the gully. I have a big scar on my left thigh as a reminder of that day and that star apple tree!

A day of fun for children in Golden River would be going to the bush, climbing trees, picking mangoes, Otaheite apples, guavas, tangerines, mangerines and going to the river to catch crayfish, if it was a good day to do so. When it rained, the river would get really wide and dirty and flow with great force, preventing humans or animals from getting close to it.

Another fun activity we used to engage in when the weather was good, and the river was calm was swimming in the river. We would make our own swimming pool by damming a section of the river. Then we would spend hours in that pool, splashing water on ourselves and on others. Afterwards, we would play marbles and hopscotch and with the toys that we had, which weren't many. I remember the toy that made me the coolest kid in the community. It was a Cabbage Patch doll that my godmother in New York had sent me. It was the hottest thing on the block! I was the only one in the community with one, so all the children converged around me, wanting to play with it.

As children, we walked barefooted for miles, often falling into potholes because the roads were bad. We used to walk miles to pick up our mail from the one post office that served all the communities in Above Rocks. Walking was the norm then. Almost everybody walked everywhere in the community, except for three families who owned cars and were related to each other.

There was no electricity at home, until I was about eight years old. To light the home at nights, we would use our lamps made of glass. We' filled them with kerosene oil and attached a wick to the burner. The wick would be lit and the flame covered with 'Home Sweet Home' lampshades. Every morning we had to clean those lampshades with crushed newspaper and get them ready for the night. Most homes in my community now have electricity. Today, those lamps are considered antiques, since they're no longer in use as much.

In addition to the outhouse or latrine, we also had an outdoor bathroom and an outdoor kitchen made of zinc. Dried wood was the fuel for the fireplace over which our meals were cooked. It was one of the jobs of the children and my grandfather to fetch wood from the forest that surrounded the homes in the community.

We also had a fire pit outside where my grandmother and grandfather cooked for the family. My grandparents taught my uncles well, because today, cooking in my family is mostly the preserve of the men. On occasions, all the cousins and neighbors would come together at my grandparents' house to "run boat" or provide informal meals for themselves.

I would eat, but I never cooked. I couldn't cook.

There was no running water at my home. People who lived near the main road had running water, but my grandparents lived in the hills. My family did not get pipes in the house until I was about eight years old. Therefore, to get water, all the kids would go to the river to tote jugs and jugs of it, every morning and every evening.

There were six shops in the community that supplied groceries. It was our job as children to go to the shop to get whatever item our family needed. We were happy to oblige, because we would get more time to play with our friends who were on similar missions for their parents. Of course, if we stayed too long at the shop, we would pay dearly.

Church

I always looked forward to going to church, and I was really integrated into it, because there were no other choices. It was our social club—the hub of the community. That was how we socialized; there wasn't much to entertain the members of the community, except for church activities.

There were three churches in the community, with the Catholic church being the most dominant. It administered the Basic school, the All-Age school and the High school. There was also a Baptist Church and the Church of God of Prophecy. I attended the Church of God of Prophecy with my family where, along with other members we would meet on Sundays, Wednesdays, Thursdays, and Fridays.

We had to walk a great distance to get to church. We walked to the end of the ridge on which we lived, which was about half a mile down a hill from our home. We then walked down another hill covered in dirt-like red clay. After that, we walked through a chocolate field, then across the first river. After crossing that river, we walked several meters before crossing another river, and after crossing that river, we walked along a rocky terrain to get to the church.

Back in those days, church services would continue for about four hours. After church, we walked home, had our dinner and returned to church for night service. After night service, we used a bottle torch to light our way back home, only to wake up the next morning to go to school.

I was no Christian then, but when it came to children's church, I was your standout kinda girl. I was involved with anything that had to do with reading and speaking. When I was very young, I used to show up in church to recite Bible verses. I also participated in Bible drills.

If something needed to be done in church, I was there. I was active in youth camps. Then, the youth of our church and some of its other branches would meet at a central location outside of our communities to fellowship by doing youth-centered religious activities.

The pastors were quite fiery and unapologetic in their ministry. As a child hearing about the wrath of God and the punishment of fire and brimstone for the ungodly, these sermons were scary to me,

Our church did not tolerate anything they viewed as sin. We had to live a godlike life as determined by the church. If members sinned, they had to go to the altar at the front of the church and repent publicly. People were also encouraged to give testimonies of God's goodness to them.

Often, the church was quick to "read" people out of the church for any of a number of infractions of the rules. Meaning they were banned from participating in the sacraments and services. So, if women or men had children out of wedlock, if women permed their hair, if women wore pants or did anything that was frowned on, they had to go. I remember being in church one Sunday for almost the entire day, glued to the proceedings as they read people out. They would call a name and a witness would testify against that person. After that "evidence" was given, the offender would be struck from the membership list of the church. They would even strike people off the membership list upon hearsay. Say they heard that an unmarried person was sleeping with someone, or a married person was sleeping with someone other than their spouse, that would be enough for these hapless sinners to be punished by being struck off the roll of the church.

Water baptism was the ritual that confirmed people as members of the church. This was a very important ritual. It declared to the world that those baptized had renounced sin, were renewed and were therefore members of the church. Members were taught about God, and that he would return to destroy the wicked with fire, not with water as he had done before. Members, and people who visited the church, were taught about hell and the need to repent to get through the pearly gates of heaven.

To make money, the church would have rallies. This was great entertainment for the people of Golden River who attended our church. People from churches in nearby communities would attend and give performances—singing and recitations. I used to sing in church and would perform at these rallies. I got many compliments on my singing. Looking back, I think they must have been hyping me up, because I no longer possess that gift! Still, those rallies were usually fun events, because my grandmother and my eldest aunt, Nellie, usually prepared wonderful meals for the people who attended, which I would enjoy.

On reflection, I think that the Church of God of Prophecy I attended as a child drew from the Baptist and Catholic churches in its practice. The major element of Catholicism that was adopted was the act of confession, but instead of repenting behind a closed area to a priest, members confessed before the whole church.

That Church of God of Prophecy has had a significant impact on my life to this day. I still believe in God. I believe in the gospel. I believe that prayer changes things, because I have seen that in the life of my mother, and in my life as well. I believe in tithing, even though I personally don't tithe. This is something that I feel guilty about, especially now that I see my little cousins who are making less than I constantly tithing. Still, I believe in giving to be able to receive, something that the Bible encourages. So I give.

From all those sermons that I listened to as a child, the idea that God is coming back with fire still lingers in my mind. But I don't observe all the teachings of the church that were impressed on me. I pierce my ears. I wear pants. I perm my hair sometimes. But I don't believe that I am less of a Christian than those people who were members of that Church of God of Prophecy church when I was growing up.

Golden River—the place, my relatives, my neighbors, friends and even the church—provided me with my first understanding of the world. When I was growing up in Golden River, that world was very small in more ways than one. We did not have much, but we didn't know that we were poor. Those were good times.

There wasn't a lot of sadness then, because my mom and grandparents did their best to keep me safe.

CHAPTER 3
MOM

SWEET POTATO PUDDING

This dessert reminds me of my mom. It's soft and sweet and comforting. It's a dessert that my relatives often made when I was growing up and one that I enjoyed then and still enjoy today.

Ingredients

½ cup unsweetened desiccated coconut (43 grams)

1 ½ pounds sweet potato (680 grams)

½ pound yam (250 grams)

3 tbsp freshly grated ginger (16 grams)

1 tsp ground allspice (2.75 grams)

1 tsp ground nutmeg (3.35 grams)

1 tbsp ground cinnamon (10 grams)

2 tbsp vanilla extract (28 grams)

2 cups coconut milk (480 ml)

¼ cup melted unsalted butter (60 ml)

¼ cup cornmeal (45 grams)

1/3 cup all-purpose flour (45 grams)

1½ cups sugar (300 grams)

2 tsp salt (13 grams)

½ cup golden raisins soaked in 3 tbsp dark rum overnight (optional)

Topping:

1 tsp ground cinnamon (3.12 grams)

½ tsp ground nutmeg (2 grams)

½ tbsp vanilla extract (7 grams)

2 tbsp sugar (25 grams)

½ cup coconut milk (120 ml)

Instructions

Preheat oven to 350°F. Grease a 10" springform pan.

Rehydrate your coconut. Soak in hot water for 15-20 minutes to rehydrate, then squeeze out all the water.

Peel all the yams, sweet potatoes, and ginger. Set a box grater, zester side up, into a large mixing bowl. Grate the sweet potatoes, yam, and ginger using the zester. This is labor intensive but gives the pudding a great texture.

Bring a cup of water to a boil in a small pot on medium-high heat. Add in the allspice, nutmeg, cinnamon, and vanilla and let boil for 2 minutes. Once this is done, pour the spice mixture into the sweet potato mixture along with the coconut milk and melted butter.

Using an electric hand mixer, combine the ingredients.

In a medium bowl, combine the rehydrated coconut, cornmeal, flour, sugar, and salt. Then slowly add to the wet mixture, continuing to use the electric mixer at medium speed until combined. (Drain the raisins and stir them in if you are using raisins)

Pour the mixture into the prepared pan and bake for one hour in the preheated oven. Remove from oven after one hour of baking time, add the topping, and then continue to cook for 15 more minutes.

A wooden skewer inserted into the center should come out clean. You will see caramelization around the edges of the baking pan, but this will not be set like a cake. The consistency will be similar to that of pumpkin pie with a stiff filling.

Let cool for 30 minutes. Use a knife around the edge of the pan and gently remove the side ring. Continue to let cool at room temperature on a wire rack for 2 hours or more, until cooled completely. Gently remove the bottom of the springform pan.

Topping

In a small saucepan boil your spice mixture. Combine all ingredients on medium-high heat and bring to a boil. Continue to boil until reduced by half. (About 10 minutes.) Remove from heat and let cool.

Like so many of her relatives before her, my mother is from a generation of people from broken homes, where fathers were missing. She knew her biological father, but he did not stay in her life for long. He left for England when she and her sister, the two children that he'd fathered with my grandmother, were very young, and then he seemed to have forgotten that he'd left them behind. The man I called my grandfather was really my step-grandfather. He was the one who, along with my grandmother, raised my mother and her sister after their father departed from their lives, in addition to their own children.

It is not surprising that the abandonment of her children and her by that man did not go down well with my grandmother. Sometimes her frustration spilled over and landed on my mother, because she was the older of the two children he'd left her with. My mom didn't complain, though. She took everything in stride as she always does and focused on making a better life than she'd enjoyed for herself and her family.

While she was attending commercial school in Kingston, she met my father, Tony Foster. He worked at a police station in Kingston. She said that when she met him, he was nice and friendly but described their relationship as a fleeting event—one of those things. As such, she does not live with any regrets about their parting of ways.

During the brief period that my parents dated, she got pregnant with me. My father was absent from her life for the duration of the pregnancy. Years later, she had another child, a son. His father, too, stayed for a short while, then left my mother to take care of his child by herself, and went on to greener pastures. Since then, I don't remember seeing my mom with a partner. She seemed to have become afraid to trust men and romantic relationships.

She had a tough life. With young children, only a high school diploma, and the fathers of her children out of her life, my mother had to think of ways to make a living. Being a go-getter, she knew her potential, and she knew the barriers that could stop her from achieving the things that she wanted to achieve in life for herself and for us. So, she worked hard to give us a stable life. Anything that she heard about that could possibly change her circumstances, she'd go for it.

Her dream was to become a nurse, and she worked hard toward getting the requisite qualification to enter nursing school. She sat and passed many subjects in the Jamaica School Certificate Examinations (JSC). The year that she finally passed all the subjects to enter nursing school, the government switched the requirements for entry from JSC subjects to subjects passed in the Caribbean Examinations Council examinations (CXC). So, my mother had another roadblock put in her way of achieving her dream.

Unable to enter nursing school, she became a pre-trained teacher. Then when the government mandated that all teachers should have at least a diploma to teach, she had to leave the classroom—another stumbling block placed in her way, one that she couldn't hurdle at that time because of her commitment as a single mother, as well as the lack of funds that prevented her from taking care of us and studying at the same time.

However, she didn't stop striving. She sewed for the neighbors, and she sewed for us. We were always well dressed. Mom used to dress me in the beautiful dresses that she made for me. I was always the child with the new dress and my hair was always tended to. That probably is one of the reasons that I love clothes, and fashion generally, so much. I am a super, super fashionista!

My mom also worked as a live-in helper. She would work from Monday to Friday and then come home to Golden River on Friday evenings. She always tried to make us feel that we weren't being left out, so on Friday evenings, when she came home, she'd bring patties for us, a treat we could barely afford. We would reheat those patties on Saturdays and our hearts were filled with joy as we enjoyed them.

When my mother was at work, I lived with my grandmother, but during the summer breaks, she would take me to her workplace in Manor Park. I would spend a couple of weeks with her in town, in the rich people's house, while she did her housekeeping. That experience opened my eyes to what was possible for me to achieve.

She eventually became a practical nurse, and that's when things changed a bit for her. She was no longer as stressed as she was before, because she could make ends meet, something she'd struggled to do in her previous jobs.

My mom believed in earning an honest bread, and she set about doing just that. I never heard her talking about doing anything shady in order to earn money. She went to work, came home, kept us fed and clothed the best she could.

When I was a child, I was happiest when I was with her. I wouldn't say that she introduced me to the finer things in life, because those did not exist for us back then. But because she worked with wealthy people and was acquainted with different foods and fruits than the ones to which we were accustomed, she would bring home a different type of food or fruit for me to try. That widened my culinary horizons. I think that was her goal, to show me that there were more options in the world than the one that I knew. And probably she was subtly holding up that life as a model for which I should aspire.

Mom, a very conscientious, soft-spoken, but firm, individual, was everything to us. She really took care of us. She gave up everything for my brother and me and gave us as much leeway as possible to express ourselves, an opportunity that I did not always take. When we misbehaved, she had her way of keeping us in line. Although she would spank us sometimes, those were rare occurrences. Because she was so soft spoken, once her voice raised an octave or two, we knew it was time to calm down!

In raising us, I wouldn't say that she led with love. She hadn't received much love, so she didn't know how to show that emotional connection, but she was always present. She led with the truth. She was quite open with us about what she was going through; she was heartbroken and lonely, having never married. But she chose to give up a social life for my brother and me. Our dads were not around, and she could have taken out that frustration on us, but she didn't. She just kept pushing even though she was struggling with us.

There was nothing that she wouldn't do for us. When I was at school, I would borrow people's money to eat lunch, and she would work it off from her sewing. Oftentimes, she did not have the money to send us to school, so she would turn to her siblings and the neighbors for money to take care of us. She was always trying to make ends meet.

My mother describes herself as a pushy mother, which is true, since she was our greatest motivator. She believed that no one was better than us or above us; they were simply more financially well off. I think she believed in us more than we believed in ourselves. Even today, she continues to encourage us to reach for the stars.

Echoing a political slogan of the seventies, many poor Jamaican parents tell their children, "Better must come." In saying this, they have hope but no understanding of how they will achieve this better, neither do they have any strategy to even achieve it. Saying better must come gives vent to their frustrations with their lives of struggle at any moment in time.

My mom did not share the better must come philosophy. Hers was, and still is, "Better *will* come", a positive assertion that her hopes and her dreams will in fact come true. And they have. The success of her children is that better that she knew would come.

Everything for us started with her. Everything started with her belief. She believed that we were going to be successes, that we were going to make her proud. So, instead of saying better must come, which suggests belief without knowing exactly how this better would be achieved, she knew that her better would come from us, and she worked hard to give us the foundation, through education, to achieve it.

She was a single mother to two children whom she sent to the best schools. I went to Campion College; my brother, St George's College. Both elite schools in Kingston.

My mother was all-seeing where I was concerned. She recognized my academic potential early, and how she nurtured it! She taught me to read at an early age, because she saw that I was special. She was adamant that I was going to be the change to her fortunes, so she kept on encouraging me.

The neighbors, probably because they didn't understand me, or for whatever reason, would make up far-fetched stories about my morals, or specifically my lack of them, which they would share with each other—rumors that even the girls in my community were skeptical about, even though we had our issues. When I heard the rumors, I would become annoyed and confused. As I walked through the community, I felt like the girl with the scarlet letter on her breast, and I would begin to doubt myself and my abilities. When those rumors made their way around to my mother, the only thing she said to me was, "Just show them. Just show them." I took that to heart, and it is still a guiding principle in my life. I adopted the belief that I would show people what I'm capable of. That is, I fight back against all negativity directed at me by "just show[ing] them" my successes.

I love my mom, and she knows that, but I was not always the obedient child that I should be, given the sacrifices that she was making for me. She'll tell people that I was a cute baby but a cheeky child.

I remember one day I came home from the University of Technology (UTech). I was tired and I hadn't eaten all day. I'd traveled home to Spanish Town from a 5:00 pm class and did not get home until 8:00 pm. When I got into the house, all that was there to eat was a little rice and corned beef that she had cooked. I knew that she had done her best, but being the brat that I was, just slammed down the pot cover. I was so hungry, and there was barely anything to eat, considering the number of mouths to be fed.

As a teen, I was really struggling, and my mom knew that. She provided the space for us to share our fears and insecurities with her, without her being judgmental. I appreciate her for that, but alas, I couldn't share all of me with her then. I lacked the voice to do so.

In spite of the challenges that she faced inside and outside the home, my mother just kept on pushing forward, sacrificing much for us and leading us by example. While she did not openly express her love for us by saying "I love you" when we were growing up, she demonstrated her love for us through the sacrifices that she made for us.

Now that we're adults, she is able to tell us that she loves us. I think this growth has occurred because she was intentional about learning how to express herself. As she ages, she has become more in tune with her emotions. She is also healing from all the trauma that she's endured, and she's let go of the negatives that have been a part of her life for a long time.

Dr. Foster, her mother Lorna and daughter K'nedy
Photo Credit: Tunde McCrown

Throughout all the struggles and the changes, she continues to choose my brother and me. When she was diagnosed with breast cancer, and as she struggled with her health, I felt like she kept choosing us, making it okay for both of us to leave her in her illness to achieve that better for ourselves and ultimately for her.

Even though she was ill, and she knew that I was charting a course without all the necessary tools, she encouraged me to go abroad. "There is no future here for you," she told me. "You can't sit here and watch me live or die." I acknowledged the truth of her words and reluctantly left her that morning, not knowing how she would survive.

But if I'd stayed, how would I have survived? The answer to that question gave me some motivation to take that plane and go. I had to give myself all the chances possible to realize the dreams for my future.

So, I left my mom in search of better.

My brother also migrated to chase his dream.

After we left, mom struggled. My brother and I couldn't help her much then. She suffered through chemotherapy, often alone. She's often told me stories about her being ill, with no one there to give her a morsel to eat. I'll be honest with you: I carry around that guilt with me. But without her selflessness, I wouldn't have been saved.

She wanted more for me than she could give me, and she set me free to chase my dreams. Her decision to let me go was what allowed me to become what I knew lived inside me, which I have since expressed through different mediums.

Lessons learned from my mom

I've learned many lessons from my mother and the life she led. I learned that you never stop being a mother, no matter how old the children get or how accomplished they become. Also, I've learned that whenever parents see potential in their children, they should always support them and try to give them the tools to realize that potential. Another lesson I learned is that we should always support our children by doing the best for them, because they might just be the ones to improve our situation in life. And, most important, I have learned the value of being independent.

My mom is always giving, even when some of those persons to whom she gives take advantage of her generosity. Like my mother does, giving to people in need is something I've been doing over the years. Unlike her, though, I refuse to allow those I choose to help take advantage of me.

Now she is battling Parkinson's disease, and she is doing it with the same resilience and grace that she has exhibited throughout all her previous struggles. She is still trying to win by exploring all her options. However, it's now our time to take care of her, but knowing my mom, will she let us?

CHAPTER 4
THE MAN WHO FATHERED ME

PEANUT CAKE

Peanut cake is a dessert that I eat, but it isn't one that I particularly enjoy. It is tough and causes me to use much effort to eat it, but it is a dessert that many people enjoy.

Ingredients

4 cups roasted peanuts

2½ cups brown sugar

3½ cups water

¼ cup grated fresh ginger

1 tsp ground cinnamon

1 tbsp vanilla

Instructions

Add the peanut and the grated ginger along with the water to a pot.

On medium to high heat, bring to a boil.

Add the sugar. Leave to cook for 50 minutes or until the liquid reduces.

Add the vanilla and cinnamon. Turn the heat down to prevent it from burning. Reduce the liquid to a sticky syrup.

Using a large tablespoon, scoop out the peanut mixture and drop it on aluminum foil or on to a singed banana leaf as we do it in the country.

Leave to cool, then enjoy.

Notes

When spooning the drops, do it quickly because the syrup starts to get hard once you remove it from the fire.

And be careful not to burn yourself with the syrup!

I didn't meet the man who fathered me until I was at university. After I was born, he visited my mother and gave her two Jamaican dollars. Two dollars! At that time, the Jamaican dollar was valued at J$1.41 to US$1.00. This means that my father gave my mother the equivalent of just over US$1.50 at that time, which is valued at about US$7.00 today. That was the sum total of his investment in my life. He made no attempt to see me after that. Probably he had written me off as one of his mistakes and had erased me from his memory. Until, that is, I chose to dredge him up. What a surprise he must have had when his past finally caught up with him!

At first, I couldn't understand why I wanted to meet him. Was it because almost everybody around me had a father in their life? Possibly. I'd asked my mother questions about him, but she didn't have too many answers. She desperately wanted to fill in those gaps in my knowledge of my father, but the truth is, their relationship had been fleeting, so she really didn't have the answers I wanted.

But, having thought about it, I think I wanted to meet him simply because I didn't want him to die without me making his acquaintance. I wanted a face that I could attach to the name. I didn't want to walk past him without knowing that I had. Plus, I had so many questions to which I needed answers, questions that were always bubbling just beneath the surface of my consciousness. Who did I look like—mother or father? What features, if any, did I inherit from my father? What was he like? Why had he been missing from my life all those years? What was his side of the family like?

Also, there was the longing for a father that I had carried around with me all my life. I wanted to satisfy that longing, because I felt that I'd missed out on not having a father, and I felt like if he met me, he would see how wonderful I was, how smart, and he would finally, *finally*, embrace me.

I knew his name, so years before I finally met him, I spent one whole week and countless hours going through the telephone directory and calling every Tony Foster listed in the book.

"I'm looking for my dad," I told each Tony who answered the phone, and I gave all of them details about my mom, hoping that one of them would remember a liaison he'd had with her.

But they all answered with one refrain, "No, I'm not your dad."

The exercise left me dejected, and I stopped searching for a while. If none of the Tony Fosters who answered the telephone was my father, then it was possible, I thought, that he was unlisted. It never occurred to me that he could be dead. I felt that he was out there somewhere, and I knew that I would meet him one day. When? I had no idea. I was just going by blind faith. I had to find him, because we had unfinished business to sort through.

Much later, I learned that my father had played my mother. He hadn't even given her his correct name. I'd wasted time and effort trying to find someone whose name I didn't even know. I'd gone on a wild goose chase looking for Tony Foster when I should've been looking for Lascelles Antony Foster. That was my father's name. But for reasons that only he knew, he'd given my mother two of his aliases, one being "Tony" a shortened version of his middle name, and the other being "Teacha," presumably the name his friends called him. A couple years after my futile attempts to find him via the telephone directory, my mother was doing business in the heart of Spanish Town, when she saw him walking out of Scotiabank.

Just like that!

She told him that he needed to meet me. He gave her a phone number and told her that I could get in touch with him at that number. I can't remember what I was thinking when we called him that night.

Probably, *Finally! I'll now get answers to all these questions that only he can answer.*

That night when we rang the number, someone answered. But it was not my father. As it turns out, he'd given us his brother Roy's phone number. Did he give my mother that number because he did not have a phone? Or, did he give it to her because he didn't want us to find him? I'm inclined to think the latter.

Uncle Roy spoke with us, and over time developed a relationship with us. He and his daughter embraced me. It seemed that fate had not intended for me to stay apart from my father and his relatives. We were destined to meet.

In fact, a few years before, I'd met one of my relatives but didn't have a clue that we were even related. When I was in sixth form at The Queens School, I started the Interact Club, the high school version of the Key Club—a social organization geared at promoting local and international connections through the projects that it implements. A young lady, Marlene Foster, was a member of the club. We were acquaintances. It turns out that she is my first cousin, being Uncle Roy's daughter. Marlene and I have developed a great friendship over the years.

I later met all my father's brothers. His mother and my maternal grandmother both had something in common—they had many boys. My father's brothers, Uncle Roy and Uncle Kat, really tried to make up for lost time. Uncle Kat was financially challenged, but he used to visit me and bring me ground provisions from Trelawny all the time. Anything he could find from his field, he would bring it to Spanish Town for me.

Now that I am grown, Uncle Kat never asks me for anything, but I feel like I should help him, so I do. I feel like I owe it to him to see that he has what he needs, because he'd done the same for me, and I thank him for all he did for me.

Through Uncle Roy, my father eventually agreed to meet me. My mom did not want him at her home, so her younger sister and I visited Bartons where we'd learned that he lived. This was a relevant bit of information to know for more than one reason: I knew where my father lived, and I knew where some of my relatives were.

I don't remember much about the journey, but I remember we approached Bartons through Old Harbour. We went to the address that we'd been given and entered the yard. Again, I don't remember much about that yard. Probably I was too focused on the idea of finally meeting my father to concentrate on much else.

A frail, short, skinny gentleman stood as we entered the property. He seemed to be nervous and unsure about how to respond to us. I was not nervous, but I was unsure about how to respond to him. He looked horrible.

What a first impression!

I felt nothing when I saw him; I had no emotions, in fact, where he was concerned. I felt no connection to him, and it was sad. He was just a blank page that I had written nothing on, and on which he'd chosen not to write anything about me. We were strangers groping around in the darkness trying to find common ground. But there was none to be found. He was my father, yes, but he'd been absent from my life for so long, I could not manufacture any feelings for him.

We made small talk for a while. He asked me about myself. I didn't ask him many of the questions for which I needed answers. I would get some of those answers later. From that visit, I learned that I had two sisters and one brother. He had two young children with his wife and another daughter he'd had from a previous relationship.

On learning that I was traveling back and forth from Spanish Town to the University of Technology (UTech) each day, he promised to pay for a room on the dorms for me. I did not have money to stay on the dorms at Utech, and I was tired from all that traveling so I was happy with his offer, and I would have appreciated that gift if it had materialized.

When the time came to pay for the room, however, I got nothing. He never showed up. He did not call, so I mentally checked out of the relationship before it even had time to develop. He stayed in the background of my life, although we had infrequent interactions over time. He visited my mother's home once. She didn't want him inside, so I entertained him on the veranda.

From these limited interactions, I also learned that at some point in his life he'd worked as a security guard at the Matilda's Corner Texaco gas station in Liguanea. The period that he worked there overlapped with the time that I attended Campion College, so it is quite possible that I'd walked past my own father a million times, going in and out of that Texaco station, without knowing that I was passing him.

I wanted my father to embrace me when he met me. Eventually he did seem to do so. Once, he did tell me that he loved me and that he was proud of me. But I realized that it was too late to hear those words, because I was already my own person. And not only was I my own person, but the damage had already been done.

I was in a place where I had gone through the hardest part of not having a father, and I was beginning to emerge as an adult who had begun to understand her role in life. I was finding out who I was, and I knew that I could manage without a father. So, nothing much changed for me when I met him. I'd got to know him, which was one of my dreams. But that was it. The wanting and the longing for a father was no longer even there. That is, not just the longing to know the man who fathered me but the longing to have his involvement in my life—to see him as a protector, a provider, a confidante, a security blanket— to see him as someone to be relied on in difficult situations. The truth is, I didn't need that person in my life again.

For a long time, I'd carried around the feeling that I wasn't worthy enough for someone to love, for my father to have stayed in my life. But, by the time I met him, I'd lost those feelings. I had other people in my life who validated me, such as my mom and friends who'd stepped in after he'd vacated his role in my life during my preteen and teen years. My self-esteem was on the rise. I no longer needed a father to validate me.

I was in his orbit for less than ten years when he fell ill. When he was declining in health and in the hospital, he sent for me. I wished him all the best, but I didn't go to see him. I didn't feel that it was my place to, so I made him wait for me as he'd made me wait for him for all those years.

He died from stomach cancer, I heard. He died waiting for me, the way I'd lived waiting for him. His responsibility was to me, to make sure I lived, but he'd abdicated that responsibility.

Yet, I felt sorry for him. I felt sorry for myself.

He'd missed out on everything—all that I'd achieved by then and all that I was on my way to achieve. He'd missed out, because he'd not invested the time in my life to share my joys with me. And he'd made me miss out on the relationships I could have had with the other children he'd fathered.

I didn't forgive him for abandoning me up until his death.

I went home for his funeral. His family had added me to the program to read a lesson from the Bible. The misspelling of my name on the program was not lost on me. It was a reminder that I didn't belong there, that I didn't belong with them. And this showed how disconnected they were from me and I from them.

I cried at his funeral. I cried for what we both had lost.

I cried, too, because it was the first time I was learning my father's real name. It was emblazoned in red below the photograph of a man decked out in a tuxedo on his death program.

My father—the unwitting motivator

Sometimes I think that my father not being in my life was actually a blessing. Even though I had my mom motivating me, I would not have had so much to prove. I would have known that I had this *one-foot-in, one-foot-out* kind of guy in my life, and that would have been some sort of comfort—stability, even. So, I mightn't have had the will to strive as much as I did.

Everything that I've been successful at, I've always had to prove to myself that I could do it. I guess because of my self-worth issues after being abandoned by my father, I always have to prove to others, whether they are in my space or out of it, that I can do whatever I set my heart on achieving. If he had not been absent from my life, I wouldn't have realized how much I didn't have, and how much I needed. I think that a lot of things that happened to me happened because he was not around. And because those things happened to me, they provided the impetus that got me going and are still motivating me to strive for even more than I've achieved so far.

Reflections on my father

What had my father wanted to tell me when he'd sent for me upon realizing that his death was imminent? This question sometimes floats around in my mind.

Did he want to tell me that he was sorry that he hadn't been there for me those years when I needed him the most?

Did he want to tell me again that he was proud of me and my achievements, even though he hadn't invested much in my life?

Did he want to tell me that if he could have lived his life all over again, he would not make the same mistakes he'd made with this one?

Did he want me to pay his medical bills?

Did he want to bequeath his family to me? I'd gotten the feeling, from a few requests he'd made of me, that he saw me as the new breadwinner for his family. But that would have been too heavy a burden, one that I was not willing to bear.

Would he have asked for my forgiveness? If he had, could I have given it to him then? I don't think so. I had too much bitterness to work through.

I was at Howard University doing my PhD when he died. I did experience a few fleeting seconds of anguish when the news of his death came. But I also remember proceeding to good old Howard China, a restaurant at the university, and enjoying my lunch, not long after.

Death is final.

It helps us put things in perspective. My father is gone, never to return. He's left his legacy behind, one open to judgment. When he died, I came to the realization that my father had lived his life his way and he'd taken his final bow.

I, on the other hand, was still here. It was my time to create my own legacy, and I couldn't go about creating the best one possible if I still held on to the pain of his abandonment. So, I've been trying to let go of that pain and bask in the joy of my accomplishments.

After his death, and having reflected on what his legacy to me was, I'd hoped that one day the legacy I would leave for the children I hadn't yet had would be superior to the one he'd left me. Now I have children, and it is even more important to me that I leave them the best legacy possible.

Lessons learned from the lack of a relationship with my father

From the lack of a relationship with my father, I've learned that girls need their dads. I missed out on that man in my life, especially in my early years. I needed to have that idea of a present father when I was growing up because I would have felt like the other children who knew their father. I would have felt whole, instead of feeling that a part of me was missing.

I believe that just as it takes two people to make a child, it takes these two people to raise a child. When I was going through the worst times of my life, I felt that if I'd had a father, he would have protected me—at least that was what I hoped.

It is often said that girls are typically closer to their fathers than to their mothers. I was robbed of that experience by my father's absence. At least I would have had the chance to prove or disprove that theory.

There were times before I met my father when I would say that I didn't need a dad, but on reflection I *did* need my father. I needed his presence in my life. When it finally came though, it was too late, because I was already an independent being. I was on my way to finding myself, and a father was not at the top of my list of priorities.

To children who are growing up without fathers who have not made it their business to be a part of your lives, know that your father not being there is not your mom's fault. More often than not, she did not send him away; he chose to stay away. Ultimately, you will be okay, but during that period of abandonment through your early years, it will be hard. It will be hard knowing that the person who should be there for you through good and bad times abandoned you.

Abandonment is not a good word, and it is a worse feeling. But just believe in your dreams. Put in the hard work to make sure that your future will be better than your present and your past, and trust your instincts. Importantly, believe that you are worthy. Stand in front of a mirror. Look yourself in the eye and know that it is not your fault that he left; none of it is your fault. You will rise above your circumstances if you prepare physically, mentally and emotionally to weather the storms of life.

Also, trust your mother. Understand that in the absence of a father, she is your protector. She is doing the best she can to give you as many of the good things of life that she can, but sometimes she will fail. Cut her some slack and help her to help you. Before you know it, you will be past the worst, and you will see your dream taking shape. And your mother will be right there to cheer you on.

Importantly, use your voice! Even though I felt that I had men in my life who could protect me, I was reluctant to trust them. I simply did not trust men. You will find that one of the reasons that you don't trust men is that your father is absent from your life. But take a chance on the good men in your life, and your mother. Give them a chance to protect you. Remember, you don't have to always try to protect yourself. I tried that and didn't do a good job of it. Instead,

I became cold and callous with my words. I would cut to pieces with my tongue anyone who dared to hurt me. I built a wall around myself that, even in my forties, there is not one person on earth who can truly say that they've penetrated that wall, that they know me.

My father shares some of the blame for this, of course, but we shouldn't live in the past. We should learn from it and keep on taking one step at a time toward the goal that we've set for ourselves. This is what I've been doing. This is what I will continue to do, no matter the challenges that I'll face. Resist the urge to build walls around yourself, because while you're protecting yourself from the hurt that is out there to make your journey to your goal more difficult than it has to be, you're also keeping in the good that you have inside that you can share with others to strengthen them on their journey.

My father has left me with much to work through. There's no denying this. He has left me with so much hurt of which I am trying to rid myself. Doing this is a process—a long slow process. I've accepted the fact that his abandonment hurt me. Deeply. But now I'm making progress in laying the past to rest.

But every so often, something happens that tickles that sore spot and resurrects the pain. When this happens, I see the situation for what it is—a test of my resolve. So, I cry if I have to, then I move on to celebrate all the good things I have in my life that the pain has not stopped me from achieving. This is a major victory for me, for which I find time to celebrate regularly. These celebrations are reminders of how far I've come and how much farther I want to go.

My father has left me with a tenacious spirit that sees every obstacle as an opportunity—an opportunity to do what others see as impossible. His absence from my life has caused me to discover hidden strengths, resilience to withstand difficulties and recover quickly from them, and determination to overcome all the challenges in my way. His absence from my life has taught me the value of quality relationships when I find them. He has shown me the kind of person that I should strive not to be. Through his irresponsibility toward me, he has inadvertently taught me responsibility.

The only tangible thing that I have left of him is one blurry picture that I screenshot from his funeral program.

So, I guess I have something to thank him for. Even in his death, he continues to help me write my story.

CHAPTER 5
FAMILY

GIZZADA

This is a totally Jamaican dessert that can be either crispy or soft on the outside, depending on how you choose to make it, and soft and flavorful on the inside with its sweetened and flavorful coconut filling. It is a family favorite.

Prep time: 10 mins
Cook time: 35 mins
Total time: 45 mins

Filling

1 ½ cups shredded coconut

1 ½ cups brown sugar

¼ tsp nutmeg

½ tsp ground mixed spice

2-inch piece fresh ginger, finely chopped

2 tbsp butter

½ cup water

½ tsp vanilla

Making the filling

Step 1: In a medium to large saucepan add the brown sugar, water, ground spice, nutmeg and fresh ginger. Once the sugar dissolves add the coconut and stir well to avoid any clumping and allow to cook for around 10 to 15 minutes, before incorporating the butter into the mixture.

Step 2: When the butter has melted, remove the mixture from the stove and prepare to fill the pastry cups.

Ingredients for the pastry

2 cups all-purpose flour

1 tsp salt

1 cup sugar

⅓ cup cold water

6 oz butter or shortening

Preparing the pastry

Step 1: Combine the dry ingredients and cut the butter into cubes.

Mix the butter and dry ingredients together either by hand or with a food processor until it resembles crumbs. Slowly add in the cold water and mix until it starts to ball. Wrap in plastic wrap and place in the refrigerator for 30 minutes to an hour to set.

Step 2: After the pastry has set, turn out onto a floured surface. Use a rolling pin to roll the dough out to a ¼-inch thickness, then use a cup, large or small to create circles by pressing the opening of the cup into the dough. Cut out circles.

Step 3: Crimp the dough. Using your index finger and thumb, pinch along the circle to create a cup shape. It will look like a starburst.

Baking the gizzadas

Preheat the oven to 350°F/120°C.

Put the pastry cups onto a pan lined with greased parchment paper, then spoon the filling into the middle of each cup. You can use your own judgment with how much or how little filling you want to add to each cup. Instructions

Bake the tarts for 20-25 minutes, then remove and let cool completely before serving.

My grandfather

To understand me, you have to get to know my family who shaped my early years and are still impacting my life today.

First, meet my grandfather, Emanuel Gilbert, otherwise known as Maas Tiny. He was actually my step-grandfather. He stepped up to parent my mom after her own father went off to England without looking back.

My grandfather was a jack of all trades. He was the best chef and was skilled at both baking and cooking—a passion he passed on to his sons. At one time, he worked at a bakery in Rock Hall. He also farmed, planting many types of foods and vegetables whenever he was not away in Kingston, working as a gardener at Manor Park in Kingston. He would travel to Kingston early every Monday morning, and we were lucky enough to see him walking home in the evening, carrying on his head the things he had bought for us.

I particularly remember the coffee, cocoa, sugarcane, yams and other ground provisions that he planted. He would roast and grind the coffee and cocoa beans, using them to make tea. It was one of my small pleasures to go to bush, his farm, with him, whenever I could. He also reared pigs, goats and chickens. Most of those would be sold to supplement the family's income. Some would find their way to the family's table.

Maas Tiny, too, was a builder. He had no choice but to build things, since he did not have the resources to pay others to do that for him, and he had to make a living. He also built homes for people in the community and in neighboring communities, as well as kitchens and outdoor bathrooms.

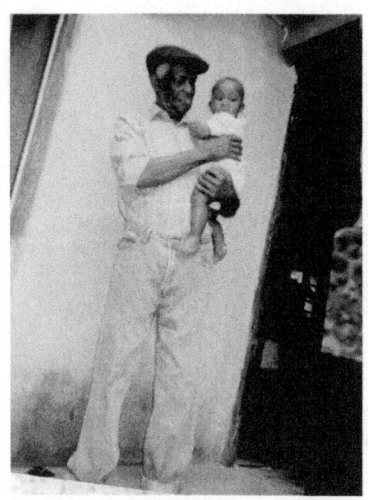

My grandfather Emmanuel Gilbert holding one of his many grand children. Photo Credit: Delroy Gilbert

My grandfather was instrumental in my life. To me, he was the best grandfather in the whole world. I don't know if it was because I did not have a father that he chose to step in to fill that gap in my life, but he made his presence felt by taking such great care of me. He made time for me, never minding when I followed him around. He was a great human being who loved his family, but, try as we might, we could never get him to put a foot through the door of a church. While my great grandmother, my grandmother and everyone else in the family would go to church, he wouldn't.

My grandfather was a bit more expressive than my grandmother. He was jovial, showed his emotions more and was friendlier than my grandmother. I remember him picking fruits and peeling canes for us. Because of his personality, all the children gravitated to him.

He was always playing with us. I'm remembering our favorite tickling game—as he tickled us and we screamed in pure joy, he would sing, "*Tunku sunku, tunku, lunku.*" To this day, I'm not sure what those words mean, but hearing them from my grandfather meant that it was time for fun.

In his eyes, we could do no wrong.

Does it sound like I had a favorite grandparent?

I did.

The boys were close to their father and would hang out with him, drinking and cooking. Whenever my grandfather was cooking, they were at the fireside with him. There was a great family dynamic, for the most part. The siblings form a close-knit group. They all get along, and I think that is a testament to how they were raised. They were all raised in close quarters—even though the family home had eight rooms, those rooms were small. But it is those values that my grandparents taught them through the lives they lived that fuel their relationship today.

My grandfather and my grandmother, Viholda Gilbert, née Gordon, took on the responsibility of helping to raise a young Altreisha.

My grandmother

Viholda Gilbert, whom everybody calls Miss Girlie, is a tall, feisty fashionista with a unique sense of style. She is skilled at crafts, and up until this day, still plaits straw and creates many beautiful works of art that she often sells to craft stores, including Things Jamaican, the premier purveyor of authentic Jamaican products and high-quality craftsmanship.

She was resilient. She had to be, considering the challenges she faced in her life, which she overcame. When I was growing up, she assumed the role of matriarch of the family and tended to the home, sharing the role of cooking with my grandfather.

She was what Jamaicans call a "war boat," that is, someone who didn't believe in turning the other cheek—though age has mellowed her. But, back then, she could give as good as she got. It didn't take much to set her off. If we got out of line, she was ready to punish us. I got several beatings from her. Beating children for punishment, in those days, was the only discipline caregivers knew. As I grew older, though, I realized that the beatings she'd given us, by today's standards, would perhaps be classified as abuse. But during my childhood—two slaps were all it took to make us fall back in line.

Oh, my grandmother could be fun when she was in a good mood. But, oftentimes, she showed zero emotion. You didn't know if she loved you or hated you, but we loved her. We still love her. She loves her boys probably more than her girls, though. She had eleven children—seven boys and four girls.

The relationship between my grandparents was a committed one, even though my grandfather was a playboy, which caused my grandmother some stress. Still, he knew how far he could go before she would set him straight.

My grandfather was not one to be romantic, but he was present in the relationship with my grandmother. They were in a common-law relationship for decades. About fifteen years before he passed, they got married. If they were experiencing any grave difficulties in their relationship, we didn't know, because they mostly hid it from us.

The truth is that while we loved our grandmother, and liked to be around her, we preferred to be around our grandfather, because we didn't connect with her as much. Which isn't to say that she didn't take care of us, however. She did. We were always happy to go spend time with her.

Four generations of Robinson-Gordon women, Dr Foster with grandmother Viholda, mother Lorna, and daughter K'nedy. Photo Credit: Tunde McCrown

Although she's always had a special love for her boys, she is still close to her girls. My eldest aunt who passed a few years ago was my grandmother's best friend. They would dress alike when they went out, and they would party together, attend funerals and set-ups together. My grandmother is close to my mother and my aunts.

From being part of my grandparents' household and having watched their relationship evolve over the years, I've learned a number of lessons that will serve me well in my own family life.

Lessons learned from my grandparents

Firstly, from my grandparents I've learned that we should never give up on our families. Regardless of the challenges being faced, always push through. My grandmother could have easily left my grandfather behind because of his philandering ways early in their relationship, but she didn't. She chose to stay and work through the challenges she faced with him. She showed perseverance and the will to compromise, weighing the benefits and risks of staying with him or leaving him. Eventually, she found that the benefits outweighed the risks. It took some time, but ultimately, they got to a place in their relationship where they accepted each other as the life partners that they were and then married to cement their relationship.

The second thing I learned from observing the relationship between my grandparents is that you can be happy without money. We had no money, but what we had was real contentment. Having money does not equate to a good quality of life. A good quality of life depends on the relationships that are built and nurtured.

Thirdly, from my grandparents, I've learned that where there is a will, there is a way. My grandparents found a way to educate their children in spite of the financial challenges that they faced to feed the family. They did what they had to do. My grandfather engaged in several endeavors to earn and take care of his family, while my grandmother stayed home and played her part. But they reaped their reward for all the hard work that they put in to raise their children. All my uncles got an education up to the graduate level, because of the encouragement from their parents. My mother's younger sister also has a graduate degree.

Aunts and uncles

I have a good relationship with most of my mother's siblings. Three of them have played a significant role not just in the family's, but also in my life.

First, there is Uncle Gifton the spitting image of his father. He's my mom's younger brother, but he was also so mature. When my grandfather passed, he became the glue that held the family together. I think he has the best personality ever. He is jovial, energetic and friendly, and the peacemaker in the family.

Second, there is Uncle Delroy. I call him Uncle Dockie, one of my favorite humans on earth. Like his mother, my grandmother, Uncle Delroy is a fashionista and steps out confidently in whatever fashionable piece of clothing he thinks shows him off best.

He is soft-spoken with a calm demeanor, is intelligent and highly educated. My uncle was super overprotective of me when I was growing up, and he was one of the first people who spoiled me. Anything I wanted, if he could afford it, he'd give me. Ironically, he was the one who brought a monster into my life, a friend of his who seemed normal the first time I met him but who would turn out to be as far from normal as possible.

These two uncles now live in Canada. They were the uncles who stood in the breach for me and became my instant protectors, the father figures in my life. My Uncle Delroy is always showing up. When the man who fathered me passed, he was my rock at the funeral—that sense of familiarity, that solid foundation in a place where everyone else seemed to be strangers.

Then there was my Auntie Mel. Soft-spoken but firm woman, Melonia Waugh who loved me, and I loved her. We would talk at length and laugh together. She was everything to me—my favorite aunt, my confidante.

She was a minister of religion in the Church of God of Prophecy, and the other doctor in the family. My Auntie Mel supported me up until the time of her death in early 2022 from a heart attack. Like Uncle Gifton, she kept the family close. Her passing is something I'm still trying to process.

From these uncles and aunt, I have learned, and am stilling learning, what it means to be a good person. Auntie Mel demonstrated that throughout her life, and my uncles are demonstrating that in their lives today.

I will always treasure the love and memories of my two dear aunts. Since my aunts Nellie and Mel's passing, I now look to my uncles for love and support.

My godmother

My godmother, Auntie Sonia, my mother's cousin, lives in New York. She's the one who'd sent me the Cabbage Patch doll when I was a child, and she sent me other things from what we would call "foreign," when she was able to do so, things like school shoes, and other school supplies. She also sent me what I like to call "sporting clothes," which were really very nice. I appreciate her for her contribution in my life.

My brother

Before my brother was born, I was the only apple of my mother's eye. I got everything—my mother's love and all the material things of life that she could afford to give me. After my brother was born, he became another apple of her eye. We got all of our mother's love and all the material things she could afford to give us. We had many toys, courtesy of the people with whom my mom used to work. I also remember my mom carving out a bit of her earnings to make toys for us. These toys enhanced our childhood and helped us create great memories.

My brother and I are very close. If you want to understand our relationship, think about Fort Knox. He has built a wall around his sister to protect her from every threat. To my brother, I'm everything. I make him proud.

To me, my brother is everything. I'd give my life for him; he'd do the same for me. If you can imagine two people living for each other, that's my brother and me. There is nothing that he wouldn't do for me, and there is nothing that I wouldn't do for him. We are each other's protectors. When he is happy, I am happy. When he is sad, I am sad.

He is a warrior. I remember someone once saying to me, "Lorna has two very smart children."

I agree.

My brother is street smart, and I am book smart. He's risen above the challenges that we faced growing up and has become an entrepreneur. Anything he touches turns to gold. Like me, he is now a parent. He became a dad in his teens, but he's made it his business to be a huge presence in his children's lives. I'm proud of the fact that he's been intentional about not just raising them, but actually being present for them. He has not forgotten his upbringing and the circumstances of his life that have made him the man he is today.

I don't know if he knows how proud I am of him. I tell people all the time that my brother is the best brother. I am proud of his successes. I am proud of how he bounces back from setbacks—I think he gets that from my mom. He can troubleshoot his way out of difficulties and shift when necessary to make good things happen for himself.

He and I experienced the worst times of our lives together. Like me, he went to high school hungry. Unlike me who had no clue where my dad was, he knew exactly where his dad was, and about the prominent position he held at his job. Yet my brother was still hungry. Imagine that!

Whenever his dad visited, while he was still just a toddler, he was miserable. He did not know how to respond to him, because he did not see him regularly. So, every time he visited, my brother would cry. He was afraid of his dad, whom he thought of as a stranger. His dad in turn was offended at his son's reaction to him, not realizing that his son's behavior was a direct result of his regular absences from his life. He may have meant well, but he used to torment my brother for being afraid of him, which in turn only traumatized my brother even more.

This, in concert with the stress that our poverty brought weighed heavily on my brother. As he grew up, he became more withdrawn. He internalized all the bad things that were happening in his life. But he chose a positive way to deal with them. He tried to drown his troubles by immersing himself in music. Often, we would observe him in a corner, quietly bopping his head.

From observing my brother's relationship with his dad, I am more convinced than ever that every child needs their father. The absence of both our dads from our lives left deep psychological scars. It seems that many men do not understand the impact that they have on their children when they abandon them.

Parents should make it their business to understand why their children are not responding to them the way they would like. They need to figure that out, and not make assumptions. For example, my brother's dad was convinced that my mom was turning my brother against him. But he did not make it his business to be a part of his son's life, to teach him anything, to bond with him. While he was basically ignoring my brother, he was being present in his other children's lives. Taking care of his other children was not a bad thing, mind you. At least he stepped up to his responsibility to them, but it seems to me that he sacrificed my brother for them.

I think his dad fell into the trap of thinking that, "Because I am your father, you have to respect me; you have to do what I say; you have to do 'this' and you have to do 'that.'" If he had built a relationship with his son, he would have gotten what he initially expected from their relationship. Like me, my brother has survived his circumstances.

Occasionally I see my brother's dad. For a while when he was in my mother's life, I used to call him dad. But everything got sour pretty quickly, because one day he was gone.

He is okay now, though.

He and my brother are getting along. That makes me happy for him and a little sad for me. Although I met my dad, I did not have a relationship as such with him. I am happy that my brother got the chance to reconcile, as it were, with his father and is working to build their relationship. It is a good example to set for his children, who, hopefully, will become good parents having grown up surrounded by good relationships from both parents and their grandparents.

Family—a reflection

The idea of a family and the knowledge that I am part of a group of people who mostly love me is a wonderful thing. But I've learned that no family is perfect. Family can love you just as much as they can hurt you. It takes a daily commitment on the part of its members to make the relationships within the family unit work.

I love the family into which I was born. I've learned that it's okay to take them in small doses when necessary. My family has improved its status over the years, but we are by no means rich in material things. What is really inspiring to me is the fact that we've come a long way from where we started in Golden River. I'm thankful for that.

A guiding principle in our family is loyalty among most of its members that transcends any difficulty we may face. My mother and my uncles believe in the benefits of family and work hard to keep the unit together. This was also the belief of my late Auntie Mel. Like my mom and uncles, she believed that it only took one person to do this. This one person must believe that family matters, and that it's worth the fight to keep it together. If such a person exists in a family, the family will stick together. My family has my mom and uncles who continue to be the glue of the family. Auntie Mel played her role as well before she passed on.

It is this idea of the importance of family that motivated my mother to pack up all her belongings and her youngest siblings and move away from Golden River. Paramount in her mind was the belief that more opportunities abounded outside of Golden River for everyone—her children and her siblings—to thrive and become the best they could be, ultimately improving their circumstances.

CHAPTER 6
LEAVING GOLDEN RIVER

TAMARIND BALLS

The tamarind ball is another Jamaican delight. For some reason, the tartness of the tamarinds and the sweetness of the sugar appeal equally to the palate of many Jamaicans. This dessert/sweet reminds me of our move from Golden River to Spanish Town.

Ingredients

1/2 cup tamarind flesh	1 cup sugar
1 tbsp boiling water	Pinch of salt

Instructions

Mash the tamarind flesh to separate the seed segments.
Add salt and boiling water to the segments.
Stir until the water is fully absorbed.
Add 1/2 cup of sugar to the flesh and mix.

Add the remaining sugar to stiffen the mixture. (Add more sugar if necessary).

Divide into small portions and roll into balls.

Leave for 15 minutes to "dry."

Roll the balls in sugar to create a dry, crunchy outer layer of sweetness.

When mom announced that she was moving to town, we were all excited. Moving from country to town is always a good thing in the minds of many people from the country. And we were no exception. Town refers to Kingston or any urban center in the parishes. Town—the place—is intriguing by itself, but the idea of town is what lures most people away from the rural areas.

When many people think of town, they think of opportunities—finding jobs, living in better homes than the ones they've grown up in, eating all kinds of foods, taking advantage of the entertainment that the city offers, among other perceived benefits. Basically, town means advancement, growth, culture and all the good things in life that people desire. We were ready to sample all the opportunities that town held out to us.

My mom is a leader, not a follower. She developed this trait, having spent much of her life raising her siblings, then raising her children. Her siblings expected her to lead. So if she said we were going to leave, everyone was ready to leave. And that's exactly what happened. She made the decision to leave Golden River, and we were ready to go with her. She was the first of the family to leave Golden River.

I was happy for my mom when she decided to leave. She needed to get out of that environment. Living there had become stressful for her. The father of her son, my brother, lived in a nearby community that she had to travel through daily to get to work. I think she was traumatized every day walking past his home, seeing the big house on that hill that he shared with his wife and children, and knowing that he was not taking care of his child. I think that was the catalyst for her leaving.

I, too, was happy to leave Golden River. Of course, I'd miss the place that I called home for eight years of my life. And I'd miss my friends and the times that we shared. I'd miss church activities, my grandparents and all the other relatives who wouldn't make the journey with us. But I wasn't sad to leave. In fact, I probably was the most excited of the family members who were ready to leave. Once I heard my mom say that we were going to leave Golden River, I felt a sense of impending growth, and I couldn't wait.

My first reason for wanting to leave was my desire to live in town. After visiting Manor Park and seeing the house that my mother's employers lived in—its furnishings, the area in which it was located and how the people lived—I wanted that life. And I thought that was the life I was heading toward. I thought that was the typical life in town.

Second, I wanted to leave Golden River because I felt that life in town was better than the life I was living in Golden River. I remembered that the food there was nice, and the place was nice. The eight-year-old me did not grasp the fact that the life to which my mother introduced me when I stayed with her in Manor Park all those summers was not my life. That was somebody else's life, and my mother was playing a critical role in their life by cleaning their home. When I visited, I was only a guest that they were simply allowing to stay in their home for a while. So, my thinking that I was going to live in Manor Park in the people's big house was a mistake. Once I'd seen better, I wanted better for myself.

The third reason for wanting to leave had to do with my ambition for myself, I suppose. I felt that I was being stifled in Golden River. As young as I was, I knew what was inside of me—I'm trying to be as humble as possible here—I knew that I was special. I believed that there were bigger things in store for me, things I could not achieve if I stayed in Golden River.

I was ready to leave.

After weeks of planning, the day finally came. Very early one morning, my mom, my mother's younger sister, their brother Uncle Xavier, and I set out on our journey. We walked to Rock Hall, a four-mile walk uphill. We trudged up that hill until our glutes started burning. We'd taken the Above Rocks, through Parks Road, past Allman Hill route. I remember the relief we felt when we finally got to the first standpipe. There we refreshed ourselves before continuing our journey. We put on our "good shoes" then. We couldn't wear them on the previous stretch of road which was unpaved and filled with holes that sometimes we had to maneuver into, sometimes around and sometimes over so as to protect ourselves from injury.

After reaching Rock Hall, I don't remember thinking, *I'm leaving all this behind.* I remember thinking, *Damn! I'm leaving!* Definitely relief. As I stood in Rock Hall that afternoon, I remembered the great experiences I'd had in town. In Manor Park. And since Manor Park was the only place in town that I'd ever visited, then it stood to reason that all of town looked like Manor Park.

At that time, I didn't know that I was poor, that the family was really struggling. I didn't quite grasp my situation, because some things in my life were good. And even though we didn't have many material things in Golden River, we'd had more than some people.

At eight years old, I lacked the words to articulate my thoughts as I am doing now. But in hindsight, these were my exact thoughts as I stood in Rock Hall that morning, ready to take the final leg of my journey to town on that big yellow country bus. After what seemed to me to be hours of travel, we finally reached town.

And what an experience awaited us! It was definitely not what I'd expected. There were no big houses with large gardens surrounded by green lawns and flowering hedges that were hidden away from the hustle and bustle of the traffic below. I was in the general vicinity of Spanish Town, not in Manor Park as I'd expected.

My mom never once told me that we were going to Manor Park. I'd just assumed that was our destination. When I didn't go to the fancy Manor Park house that I'd set my mind on, I was surprised and a bit disappointed. But I was also happy, because I was here. I was finally in town. I wasn't to know it yet that a mixed bag of experiences awaited me, some that would break me and some that would cause me to flourish.

CHAPTER 7
SPANISH TOWN

CORNMEAL PUDDING

Cornmeal pudding is one of those easy-to-make and cheap desserts that was a staple in my family while growing up. It's said that cornmeal staves off hunger and cleans out the body. It certainly staved off the hunger when we were able to have it!

Ingredients

3 cups cornmeal

1 1/2 tsp salt or salt to taste

1/2 cup flour (all-purpose or regular flour)

1 tsp grated nutmeg or ground nutmeg

1 1/2 tsp ground cinnamon

6 cups coconut milk

1 tbsp vanilla extract

1/2 cup (1 stick) butter (optional)

2 cups brown sugar

Note: You may add raisins or any other ingredients that you desire, but when I was growing up, we only used the basic ingredients above (without the butter).

Ingredients for soft top

1 cup coconut milk

1/2 tsp ground cinnamon

1/4 cup brown sugar

Instructions

Preheat the oven to 350° F. Grease a 10-inch baking pan. Set pan aside.

In a medium-sized pot, add the coconut milk, butter (if using), brown sugar and vanilla extract and heat on medium heat. Mix until the sugar is dissolved, and the liquid is heated but not boiling. Remove from the heat and set aside to cool.

Sift all the dry ingredients: flour, salt, nutmeg, cinnamon and cornmeal in a large mixing bowl. Whisk together, until combined.

Pour the warm liquid on to the dry ingredients and mix well with a whisk or a wooden spoon. Continue to whisk for a few minutes to make sure it is smooth.

Pour the mixture into the greased baking pan.

Bake for 20 minutes first. In the meanwhile, whisk the ingredients to make the soft top in a small bowl.

Remove the pudding from the oven and pour the soft-top mixture over the top of the partly set batter and bake for 80 minutes. The top of the pudding will be soft, while the bottom will be firm when it is done.

Allow it cool for about an hour. Enjoy.

Spanish Town was an eye-opening experience for me. It was nothing like Golden River with its lush greenery, dirt roads, houses being few and far between, and a highly developed community spirit. Neither was it like Manor Park with its huge homes, well-maintained lawns and well-tended hedges. It was…different, but it was okay.

When I moved to Spanish Town with my big hopes and dreams, I actually liked the place. The hustle and the bustle was like nothing I'd experienced in the laid-back community of Golden River, but it was exciting. What was harder to come to terms with were the unpleasant, smelly drains that seemed to be a feature of the landscape there. These are the potent memories I have of home in Spanish Town.

I was in Spanish Town when Hurricane Gilbert hit Jamaica in 1988. I remember the rising water in the backyard. As the zinc roof lifted, the water rose and rose. We lived next-door to an untended drainage system that overflowed with the slightest of drizzles. I survived Hurricane Gilbert, but there would be many other hurricanes in my life.

The first house we lived in was one off Old Harbour Road. It was alright, nothing special. We lived there several months, but within a year we had moved to Ensom City, a middle-class community, on the outskirts of Spanish Town. Six of us shared a house: my mom, Uncle Delroy, my brother, my mom's younger sister, and her boyfriend who would later become her husband and a bane to my spirit.

Civil servants, like teachers, nurses and policemen, lived in Ensom City when I lived there. The children were mostly from two-parent households, and many of them were my age or older, so we all socialized together. Having the companionship of all these children made Ensom City a good space for me.

The community was quiet and great for families. My extended family fit right in. But somehow, I always felt that I didn't quite belong there. And I was right. I'd had some good times in Spanish Town, but there had also been some really bad times. Toward the end of my stay in Spanish Town, I'd grown to hate it there. I left and didn't want to look back.

My mother's younger sister's boyfriend had not lived with us in the house off Old Harbor Road, but he'd been there all the time. They, as good Christians, were disguising their carnal relationship under the guise of being just good friends. When we moved to Ensom City, however, he moved in, something I wished that he hadn't done, because he would become one of those other hurricanes I had to endure and overcome.

CHAPTER 8
EDUCATION IN JAMAICA

PANNA COTTA

Panna Cotta is not a Jamaican dessert, but it is one that I wished I could have enjoyed in Jamaica in my preteen and teen years. But I know that we couldn't have afforded it then. It is a warm comforting dessert that reminds me of relaxation. The Panna Cotta is a revered delicacy that's mostly consumed in the homes of the upper echelons in society. This dessert is a metaphor of my life. My education has allowed me to be among the most revered among us, and I was educated among the richest and brightest in our country.

Ingredients

⅓ cup skimmed milk

1 (.25 ounce) envelope unflavored gelatin

2 ½ cups heavy cream

½ cup white sugar

1 ½ tsp vanilla extract

Instructions

Pour the milk into a small bowl. Sprinkle the gelatin powder over the milk and stir until combined. Set aside.

Stir heavy cream and sugar together in a saucepan. Set over medium heat and bring to a boil; watch it carefully, as the cream can quickly bubble up and boil over.

Immediately stir the gelatin mixture into the boiling cream, stirring until completely dissolved. Cook and stir for 1 minute.

Remove the pan from the heat and stir in the vanilla.

Pour cream mixture into 6 individual ramekins. Leave to cool, uncovered, until no longer warm, about 20 minutes.

When cool, cover with plastic wrap. Refrigerate until set, at least 4 hours but preferably overnight.

The early years

I'd left Golden River in grade 4 and had two more years of primary school to complete. That was not an issue for my mom and me. I was smart, so I was sure I would fit in. Many people had seen my potential before I had, but once I'd recognized it, there was no stopping me.

My mom was the first person to tell me that I was smart. She said that I was a very smart toddler. I walked early. I talked early and I was reading books from I was about two and a half years old. By the age of three, I was reading everything I saw, and I was putting letters together to form words. That's when she realized that I was really gifted. My favorite book was *Talisman and the Goat* written by Laura Facey and published in 1976. That book has forty-seven pages. I had that book for a long time and read it many times before I attended basic school.

My earliest memory of school is September 6th, 1983. I'm not sure why I remember that date, but it sits on my hippocampus. I believe it was my first day of basic school in Above Rocks. The Catholic Church was the basic school. It was a concrete structure painted blue that rested on a ridge below the post office. There were two classrooms, and I felt like we were in a dungeon. Apart from these basic facts, I don't remember anything about my performance there.

At six years old, I left the basic school and went to St Mary's All-Age School in Above Rocks. I stayed there until the end of the fourth grade. To get to school, I had to walk to the bottom of the ridge on which I lived, then I walked another half-mile downhill on a road covered with red clay-like dirt, before walking through the chocolate field, then across a river. After crossing that river, I walked several meters, crossed another river, then walked up a winding mountain road until I reached the main road. After that, I'd walked two miles along the main road until I got to the big river that overflowed its banks when it rained. After crossing that river, I walked another half-mile up another hill that led to the school. To get to the school from the top of that hill, I walked down an incline on a winding staircase that led to the school through a cemetery.

That was my regular route to and from school each day. If it rained, I had to walk an additional three miles along the main road because going across those rivers, which shortened my journey, would have been suicide.

While I remember my journey to school well, I don't remember much about being at St Mary's. I remember that I wore a blue tunic and white blouse. I remember that we sat at wooden desks that seated four children, and I remember that it used to be hot on the playing field.

I don't remember if they placed students according to academic performance each year. But I remember that when I was six and had just started all-age school, my mom told someone that one day I would attend a school with the children of the prime minister and other important people.

That person laughed in her face. Their reaction to her prediction did not dissuade her from "bigging me up" every chance she got. She told me that I would be on interview programs one day. While I did not understand what she was talking about, I believed in my academic acumen. I knew I had something.

When I did the *Television Jamaica* interview with Simone, all those years later, and she told me the interview was my profile, I smiled, because my mother's words came back to me in that moment. I really think what my mom was doing throughout my childhood was encouraging me to challenge myself, to believe that I was good enough.

It worked.

When we moved to town, I traveled to school in Kingston each day. My mother's younger sister taught at Clan Carthy Primary School, and my mother worked outside of Spanish Town. My mother decided that it was best to go to the school where her sister taught, so that I would have a guardian throughout the day.

I started Clan Carthy Primary School in grade 5 and spent two years there. There were several differences that I immediately noted between St Mary's and Clan Carthy. At St Mary's, I knew everybody. There, I was used to sitting at desks that seated four children. Those desks were wooden and had carved-out pencil holders at the top. At Clan Carthy, I had my own desk.

I remember thinking, *These town people have it really good!*

I was really excited to be in town and at that school. As far as I was concerned, life in town was better than it was in Golden River—at least as far as nice material things were concerned.

I did very well at Clan Carthy, even though I was often tired, having to take the bus from Spanish Town to Vineyard Town every school day and traveling back home in the afternoons. When it was time to sit the Common Entrance Examination, I had to choose schools I would prefer to attend. The way this works is that the children who were sitting Common Entrance—the primary school exit exam at the time—were given the option to choose about four high schools that they preferred to attend, if they passed the examination. We had a first choice, second choice, and so on. For some reason that I don't remember now, I picked Campion College as my first choice.

My mom was not particularly supportive when I told her that I had chosen Campion College. It wasn't that she doubted my ability. Not at all. She'd always believed that one day I would go to school with the children of important people, and those were the children who attended Campion. But the truth is, she was not completely sold on the idea of me going there. Probably she understood the culture shock that awaited me there, and she knew what going there would do to my innocence, and that made her anxious.

But her sister, the Clan Carthy teacher, told her to let me choose the school I wanted to attend. So, I stuck with Campion College, choosing Immaculate Conception High for second. The other choices? Honestly, I do not remember.

The morning when the Common Entrance Examination results were published, I was in Spanish Town square by the Texaco gas station, across from the shopping center. My mother and I were waiting on a bus to go to Kingston. She bought a newspaper, and we scrolled hastily through it until we found the section with the list of names of students who'd sat Common Entrance and the schools in which they were placed. We found my name—Altreisha Foster. No middle name. No Nass-sheva.

I'd passed for Campion College! I was so excited. My mother was excited. I went to school feeling like a *hot girl*. When I got there, however, there was no special celebration for me, but my teacher was overjoyed. When students passed their Common Entrance for good high schools, all the adulation goes to the teacher. The quality of her passes will brand her as a great Common Entrance teacher, and her status in the school will rise.

My teacher's star shone brightly that day, as she had many great passes, but mine topped them all. My uncle, my mother's youngest brother, was also in my class. He had passed for St George's College. There would be a great celebration for us when we reached home.

Later that day, I learned that the daughter of one of the teachers at Clan Carthy had also passed the examination for Campion College. Like me, she was a bright spark, but she attended a preparatory school, just across the way from my school. Imagine how elated I was that, even though I had attended a regular primary school, my performance had matched that of one of that school's top students. In fact, two children from that school were placed at Campion; I was the only student from my school who had been placed there. I had done well. From a government school with fewer resources than preparatory schools, there was one student going to the top high school in the island at that time! Me!

Although at school I was not feted for my achievement, I thought that my teacher was happy about my success. But, apparently, she'd doubted my ability. The ten-year old me had never doubted *my* ability. I'd constantly reminded myself that I could excel. I'd worked hard to excel and *had* excelled. I'd deserved my achievement. But my teacher obviously thought differently!

After I finished first form at Campion, I remember a conversation I had with my best friend from primary school, who was then attending the Convent of Mercy (Alpha Academy). She told me that our grade 6 teacher had expressed doubts about my ability to perform academically at Campion and had told them that I was doing badly there. I wondered who'd given that teacher that bit of news. My heart was broken because I thought that my teacher had really believed in me, but I was even more heartbroken that she'd repeated the gossip as if she'd believed it.

Now that I think about it, I believe the teacher had looked at me and had seen poverty and equated that poverty with what we Jamaicans term *dunceness*—low intelligence. In her mind, I did not fit the mold of people who should be bright. So, she'd discounted all of my effort, even in spite of my great performances in her class, and had relegated me to the pile of children she'd deemed to be unimportant—the ones who were not destined to make good of themselves.

She believed whatever she'd heard about me, without using her critical thinking skills to question the truth, which she should have done since I'd been one of her best students. Tragically, that teacher would not be the first adult to doubt me and treat me with disdain. I would meet them soon enough.

After hearing what she'd said about me, I told myself that I was not going to be a victim of her prophecy. I did not believe her. I believed in the prophecy of my mother who saw me rubbing shoulders with important people. And I had my own dream for my life. I was going to be a success, and education was going to be the key to that success.

That teacher's perception of me had riled me up, and I was determined to show her that I could be anything that I'd wanted to be, and I was going to be good at what I'd chosen to do.

High School—Campion College

The first morning of high school, I went decked all my school finery and accessories, thanks to Auntie Sonia, my godmother, who made sure that I started school on the right footing. When she'd heard that I had passed my Common Entrance, she was elated. She'd known me when I was a baby, and she knew that I was smart, so she tried to help me whenever she could.

The commute to Campion from Ensom City was taxing. I traveled approximately seventeen miles each way every day. This did not affect my academic performance, though. My first two years there were great academically. I excelled. I placed second in my classes, then I was a top five performer in subsequent years up to fourth form.

But it wasn't long after I started attending Campion that I realized that my family was dirt-poor. When I lived in Golden River, I'd been super protected. I did not perceive the difference between the haves and the have-nots. To my mind, everybody had shared the same economic status. And even though my mother had introduced me to the life of the wealthy in Manor Park, I did not feel that I didn't belong there. I felt at home. My mother's employers did not discriminate against us, and because they'd treated me well, I'd thought of myself as any other child, happy and with dreams.

But I was poor! My mom could not afford to replenish my stock of school supplies as I outgrew them or when they fell apart. For example, my shoes would squeeze sometimes. I have a persistent bunion on my right mini toe today as a reminder of those unfortunate times. To keep me in socks to maintain the school's dress code she would sew two pieces of old socks together to ensure that the white was always on the top. Sometimes she would sew a brown addition inside to the white to extend the toe. This bit was always hidden in my shoes.

I was often hungry. Oftentimes I would walk to Mr. Binn's office to collect the coins he had collected from the student donations to supplement my lunch money. It was my walk of shame. The pressure of not having much and watching others with so much almost destroyed me, and it forced me to hide the real me. I was often sad. Now I know that I was suffering from depression. That's when I began to grow my shell.

Campion College was a completely different world from the one I'd known. There were many rich children going to that school, and I did not fit in. Imagine a child who is poor, going to a school with the children of politicians and other important people, having to squeeze into a bus to get to school and getting there hot and bothered. I would see the parents driving around in the parking lot in their Mercedes Benzes and other luxury cars, and sporting other forms of luxury, say, something that could be as small as a simple igloo in order to have cold water during the school day. For me, it was stressful, knowing that my peers were going to be picked up by their parents, or their drivers, at the end of the school day. It would take them probably five minutes to get home. Meanwhile I had to struggle on the bus for hours before reaching my home. I also felt peeved that they could do whatever they wanted to do without counting the financial cost. Knowing my circumstances, these realizations took a mental toll on me.

I was living in a world that I did not know; a world in which I had no clue about how to exist. I didn't have the tools I needed to be successful in that world. I didn't know how to thrive at Campion College. I lacked the cultural capital—identified by the French sociologist Pierre Bourdieu and his peers as being necessary for success at school. My family lacked the economic resources and the behaviors displayed by those who did. I hadn't been schooled in the norms of middle-class society. That was something I would later learn.

I did not come from a family where educational achievement was on display, although it was highly encouraged. I wanted it, not just because my mother saw my potential and tried to nurture it. I wanted it for me. I was well read, and Standard English was my everyday register, but that did not count for much when I lacked the other symbols and behaviors of the privileged.

I know that I was not the only poor student at Campion College at that time. Probably, if I'd grown up in town, I would have learned how to navigate the social relationships and the behaviors on display there. But I'd only been in Spanish Town two years, with my culture from Golden River still embedded in me—a culture that was light years from that displayed by many of my peers at Campion College. I was out of my depth there.

I don't know that more than a handful of people at Campion College understood me. I certainly didn't understand most of them. I know that my socioeconomic situation was a huge barrier between me and members of the school community—at least from my viewpoint.

I didn't live up to my potential at Campion College. Fifth form was rough. I was hungry some days and fatigued on others, and this eventually caught up with me after seven years of traveling to school without having enough to eat and not getting enough rest. I didn't have the energy to study. My long commute from home to school and back, which was exhausting, my lack of adequate amounts of food in the quantity and quality necessary for my mind to function optimally, and certain traumas I was enduring at the time accounted for my relatively poor performance at Campion. As such, I left school with fewer subjects than I had expected and didn't make it to sixth form, even though students with the same number of subjects that I'd passed and quality of passes that I'd gained had made it. I wondered about that.

I agree that smart children, whether from rich or poor homes, should go to the best schools where there are resources to help them develop their abilities. But the best schools are the ones that the children of the middle class and the rich usually attend. When ultra-poor students meet with the ultra-rich in the school setting and peer pressure takes over, the negative psychological effect that can have on poor smart kids is far-reaching.

Having made this observation, I realize that there is still much for which I should thank Campion College. This school provided me with the resources to comprehend what I wanted from life and to plot and chart the trajectory of my life. It provided me with resources such as knowledge, attitudes, behavior, worldview, and friends that would prove invaluable to me as I tried to find my place in the world. Without these resources, I would have had a more difficult time than I've had in taking advantage of the opportunities that have come my way.

My stint at Campion College helped me to appreciate the finer things in life and reiterated the value of education. I realized that the only way for me to achieve the things that many students at Campion College took for granted was to work hard to put myself in a position to achieve them. So, after having thought about my experiences at Campion College, I can say that it is one of the catalysts of my success.

High School— The Queen's School

For sixth form, I went to The Queen's School, a high school for girls. There I studied subjects that I hoped to sit at the Advanced level (A-level). But Queen's was really a steppingstone, a placeholder for me. I could have gone to the University of Technology, Jamaica (UTech) straight out of Campion College, but I didn't believe I was mature enough.

School was good at Queen's. I performed well on assignments and on tests and eventually sat the external exams. However, what no one knows to this day is that I never got my A-level results from Queens. I could not get my grades because I owed thousands of dollars in outstanding tuition.

None of that mattered, though, because I was accepted to the University of Technology, Jamaica based on other merits.

University of Technology (UTech)

At UTech I studied Medical Technology. I chose to do that program because of its name. I'd always wanted to do medicine, and the program was as close to medicine as I could get at that time. When I'd looked at the Medical Technology curriculum at UTech, there were a lot of science-based courses, which intrigued me. I'd always known that I would pursue a career in the sciences. So, in preparation for this, I'd focused on the sciences in high school. It was easy for me to choose a career in the sciences, because, like many other Jamaican children, I'd been socialized to think that I had to become a lawyer, a doctor or an engineer to rise out of poverty. I was therefore laser-focused on mastering one of those professions. It would be my ticket out of poverty. In charting my path to success, science, and anything in that field, was the way to go.

Had I better understood the medical technology program before applying to UTech, however, I think I would have chosen to enter the School of Pharmacy instead. But I did not know that such a school even existed until I went to UTech. So, based on my available knowledge of the courses offered then, I thought Medical Technology was the best move. Still, I was able to use this course as a steppingstone to get closer to what I wanted to do. Had I done Pharmacy, I would have had to do over my entire undergrad when I ended up at Howard University, but this time in Biology, and then apply to their School of Pharmacy.

When I chose to do Medical Technology, my goal was just to be employed. I knew whatever I did would have to be a skill-based degree—*that* I was confident of—so that when I graduated, I was going to move into a profession.

Initially, my career goal was to be a neurosurgeon like Dr Ben Carson. He was doing great work in his field, and I admired him.

I wanted to emulate him. He was my role model for a long time, until he decided to enter the political arena. His political career did not show him in the best light, so my one-sided love affair with him ended. Finished. Over. Kaput! His books are great, though.

In addition to my studies at UTech, I was involved in extracurricular activities such as dancing and cheerleading. Who knew I'd become a social butterfly in spite of the challenges that I was facing in my personal and school life? But the truth is, my social life allowed me to put the reality that I was living on the back burner for a while. It relieved some of the stress that I was under daily. It reminded me that I had friends, that I was part of a larger group than the one into which I was born, and that I could contribute to this group. These social activities provided an escape for me from the weightier matters of my life with which I was having difficulty coping.

At UTech, I wasn't focusing on my studies. I was traveling from Spanish Town to Papine, retracing the route I'd taken to Campion College, but this time going farther. I was hungry, tired and broke most of the time. Of course, nobody could tell that I was suffering. At one point I was so depressed, I felt like my body was shutting down, and I was becoming incontinent. I could not understand it. And I did not seek medical attention.

To relieve some of the stress, I'd ask my friends to stay with them. They agreed, but that situation wasn't ideal. They had their own challenges to deal with, and my presence in their space only added to their frustration and mine. I was absolutely depressed, so depressed that I neither had the energy nor the will to cope with schoolwork.

I was failing and almost expelled from UTech for underperforming. Were I to be expelled, that would have really derailed my life, I knew. Once again, dear Auntie Mel came to the rescue. She intervened on my behalf and advocated with the dean that she should give me a fourth or fifth chance to prove myself, instead of acting rashly. Thankfully, the dean accepted her reasoning, and I got a reprieve.

Dr Eugeny Brown was that dean. At the time, she was Dean of the Science Department, and she was also a pharmacist. When I stepped into her office, she looked at my grades, then she looked at me. "I know that you know better than this," she told me pointedly.

"I know that you can do better than this. I've heard that you can do better than this. So go and do better."

After her pep talk, she gave me the registration slip and told me to register for my classes over the summer. I did and passed all the classes over the summer break. I had four or five classes that I had to pass. She gave me the opportunity to prove myself and for that I am grateful, because I could not have carried those classes into the following year while doing a full schedule of classes.

Dr. Brown saw my potential and forced me to turn my life around, so I was able to move from almost getting expelled from UTech to graduating with second-class honors. Dr. Brown would turn out to be one of my guardian angels I'm honored to have had in my life.

CHAPTER 9
THE MCLEODS

BREAD PUDDING

Bread pudding was Dad's favorite dessert—Dad being Trevor McLeod who adopted me and welcomed me into his family. He loved his bread pudding just as how he loved and supported me. I will honor him in his absence by sharing his recipe here.

Preparation time: 20 minutes

Cooking time: 45 minutes

Ingredients

8 slices hard dough bread or any dense bread

4 tbsp butter

1 cup raisins (more or less to your desired taste)

½ cup granulated sugar

½ tsp salt

½ tsp cinnamon powder

½ tsp allspice

4 large eggs

2 cups whole milk

1 cup evaporated milk

Note: You may use 3 cups coconut milk or any other plant-based milk that you have if you do not use dairy.

Instructions

Butter one side of each slice of bread.

Grease 9" baking dish with butter.

Tear the buttered slices of bread into small pieces and arrange them in a layer at the bottom of the dish.

Sprinkle some of the raisins on that layer. Cover that layer with more pieces of bread. Sprinkle raisins on that layer. Continue to create layers and cover each layer with raisins to almost the top of the pan. Top last layer with raisins.

Combine granulated sugar, salt, cinnamon powder, allspice, eggs and milk, mix until the sugar has dissolved.

Pour the mixture over the bread and raisins and allow to rest for 15 minutes.

Bake in a preheated oven 190°C (375°F) until the bread pudding is browned on top or when a knife inserted in the center comes out clean.

The McLeods. God bless the McLeods! They are members of a troupe of guardian angels that played central roles in my life.

At Queen's, I met a young lady by the name of Tremone. She'd attended St. Andrew High School for Girls, and, like me, she didn't matriculate into her school's sixth form. I think it was because we were both imports into The Queen's School that we gravitated to each other. Since she didn't know anyone there and I only knew one other person from Campion College who, like me, had chosen to do sixth form at Queen's, we became instant friends and have maintained a deep lifelong friendship.

We would do extra classes in A-level Math and Chemistry at Holy Childhood High School. She had a driver who would take her to the Math class and oftentimes I would hitch a ride with her. Doing extra classes at Holy Childhood High School was good for me, because it was at a central location, so it was much easier for me to get my bus to go home after classes. Man, I needed those extra classes, but I just couldn't afford to pay for them. I was doing my best to continue the classes, but my mom was only able to pay a little bit here and there. She was still trying to give me what I needed to move ahead, even though she found it challenging.

One day when I returned home from school, my mom told me that Tremone's mother, Andrea, had called her. Tremone would often speak to me about her mom, whom I'd met only a handful of times. So, I was quite perplexed. *What the hell did I do? Had I done something to offend Tremone and she'd got her mom involved?*

I couldn't think of any reason why Tremone's mom should have called mine. Tremone and I had spent that day under the ackee tree—our hangout spot at Queen's—and we'd parted amicably at the end of school. So busy was I running possible scenarios through my mind that I almost missed what my mom was saying: Tremone's mom had paid all my back fees for extra lessons, and she had promised to pay for all my extra lessons going forward.

I was shocked. Before I could let what I had heard sink in, my mom told me that Tremone's mom had gone on to suggest that I stay at their home during the week, so that I wouldn't have to take the bus home every evening. She would take me home at the end of each week.

Oh, such sweet relief! I can't remember if I laughed or cried. But I was really happy. A huge weight had been lifted off my shoulders, and I'm sure that my mom felt the same way. She no longer had to pay two school fees for me. Neither did she have to provide breakfast, lunch and dinner for me for five days of the week.

We accepted the offer, needless to say. I would leave home in Spanish Town for school on a Monday morning with all that I would need for the week, and at the end of the school day I'd go to stay with the McLeods.

The first thing I noticed before long, and which I proved over the entire time I stayed with them, was that the family was a happy unit, and they weren't afraid to show it. They were playful, and they communicated well with each other. Trevor and Andrea McCleod were, at the time, both in leadership positions at telecoms giant, Cable & Wireless, now LIME.

Tremone and I shared a room, but I had my own bed. At their home, I lacked nothing—food, clothes—whatever they thought I needed, they gave it to me. I could eat anything I wanted in their house, and I could sleep anywhere I wanted. There was no place in that house where I couldn't go. Her parents really took very good care of me. They treated me well; I was their third child.

They didn't owe me or my mom anything. They didn't know us. They didn't have to take me in. I used to wonder why they had chosen me, until Mrs. McLeod pointed a finger at her daughter, Tremone. As she tells the story: Tremone aka Tokie had told them that her friend, Altreisha, was coming to stay with them, no questions asked. And that was that.

This does sound like my Tremone; that's how much I know she rides for me. Tremone saw that I was struggling and dumped me, as it were, on her folks, and they did not shirk that big responsibility that Tremone had imposed on them. They knew that I was their daughter's friend, and they reached out a helping hand. Since day one they called me their daughter, and I am forever their daughter. I called them Mom and Dad.

Andrea McLeod is a beautiful fashionista. She would get regular manicures and pedicures, and she treated me to these as well. We used to visit a nail salon in York Plaza in Half-Way-Tree. The things my mom could not afford to do for me, she did. When Tremone got her hair done, I got my hair done as well. She introduced me to a life that I did not yet know.

I am still close to the family. When Tremone and I are apart, time seems to stand still, and once we're together again, it's as if we had not parted. Mr. McLeod has since died, but when he was alive, anything I did well, any form of success I had, he and his wife would celebrate with me. My success was their success.

Mrs. McLeod still supports me today by celebrating my wins. I am indebted to the family. They were my angels at a time when I most needed angels. I'll be forever grateful to them.

If the McLeods had not chosen to help me my life would have been much harder. They gave me everything and asked for nothing in return. They just wanted to give me the best chance to realize my potential that they must have thought I possessed.

This is one of the reasons why I believe in tithing and praying. This is something my mother always did. I believe that's one of the reasons that guardian angels were sent into my life. Because of the McLeods I didn't have to spend a lot of time in Spanish Town where I felt I was being buried alive.

The McLeods' selflessness has inspired me. The McLeods can take some credit for pointing me to one way that I could help others who have potential to do well but do not have the

Mr. Trevor McLeod
Photo Credit: Family archive
Tremone McLeod

means to do so. Because they and the other guardian angels in my life had done so much for me, I was motivated to mentor girls who are experiencing similar traumas to the ones I endured when I was their age. It is wonderful to receive but it is more wonderful to give, as I've been realizing.

CHAPTER 10
LEAVING JAMAICA

STRAWBERRY CHEESECAKE

I see the knitted eyebrows, and I can already hear the questions: "Cheesecake? Why cheesecake?" The cheesecake represents my rebirth. The quality of my life changed at this point. It was a pivotal change and represents sweetness for me—the sweetest part of my journey through life at that moment.

Base of Cheesecake

200g/7oz graham crackers

8 tbsp unsalted butter, melted

Cheesecake filling:

1 lb/500g cream cheese, softened

1/2 cup sour cream (your preference)

2 tbsp all-purpose flour

1 1/2 cups caster sugar

1 tsp vanilla extract

Zest of 1 lemon

3 eggs, at room temperature

Strawberry topping for cheesecake:

500g/1 lb strawberries, half-diced and half-halved

2 tbsp lemon juice OR water

1/2 cup white sugar

1/2 tsp vanilla extract

1 1/2 tsp corn flour/cornstarch

2 tbsp water

Instructions

Preheat oven to 160°C/320°F (standard) or 140°C/295°F (fan/convection).

Get a 20 cm/8" springform cake tin. Turn the base upside down, butter lightly and place a square piece of parchment/baking paper on the base. Then clip into the springform pan—excess paper will stick out.

Butter and line the side of the pan.

Cheesecake biscuit base:

Roughly break up biscuits by hand and place in a food processor.

Blitz until fine crumbs. Add butter, then briefly blitz until dispersed and it resembles wet sand.

Pour into the prepared cake tin. Use a spatula to roughly spread it out over the base and up the walls.

Use something with a flat base and vertical edges almost to the top of the sides and flatten the base.

Filling:

Use a mixer or beater to beat the cream cheese until smooth.

Add flour, beat until incorporated.

Add vanilla, sour cream, sugar and lemon zest. Beat until combined.

Add eggs, one at a time, beat in between until combined, and after the last one, beat just until the egg is fully incorporated.

Pour into prepared crust.

Bake for 55 minutes. The top should be a very light golden brown, smooth and almost perfectly flat, jiggling slightly when pan is gently shaken.

Cool the cake in the oven with the door open, then refrigerate for at least 4 hours in the pan.

Remove sides and slide cheesecake off the cake pan. Then slide the cheesecake off the paper.

Strawberry topping for cheesecake:

Place chopped strawberries, vanilla, sugar and lemon juices in a saucepan. Stir then bring to simmer over medium heat.

Simmer for 10 minutes until strawberries breakdown.

Mix corn flour with water, then add to saucepan and stir.

Add halved strawberries and cook for 1 minute to soften.

Sauce should be syrupy. Remove from stove and cool until thickened a bit.

Once cool, stir. Adjust thickness to make it the right oozing consistency, if necessary, with a tiny touch of water.

Spoon onto cheesecake so it's covered with a single layer of strawberries. Flip strawberry halves so they are face down. Refrigerate for at least 2 hours.

Slice and serve with remaining strawberry sauce!

After I left UTech, I had to do an internship as part of the requirements that I needed to complete to be granted a license to practice as a medical technologist. The summer after I graduated, I immediately started working at the Annotto Bay Hospital in St Mary. I did not see myself going home to Spanish Town. I just could not see myself moving back to that place. That's how traumatizing living in Ensom City had been for me, so after my internship, I did not go to Spanish Town.

I completed my internship at the Cornwall Regional Hospital in Montego Bay, St. James. That done, I still couldn't even look in the direction of Ensom City. I went back to Annotto Bay, this time for a summer job. From the money I earned from my internship, I was able to contribute toward paying the bills at home, and I even started paying back my student loan. I also bought a stereo for my mom. Since I was working and had some money, I wanted the house to look and feel different. However, I was not earning enough even though I had a professional degree, so I could barely make ends meet.

I knew instinctively that I could do better. But the life I wanted was not possible in Jamaica, because I did not have the resources to invest into creating that life. I'd seen my friend Marsha leave Jamaica and was doing well for herself in the USA. She was thriving, and she had encouraged me to follow in her footsteps.

I considered her suggestion. I needed to go somewhere, I decided, somewhere I could start to thrive as well. I would take the opportunity that Marsha had been holding out to me by going to study in the USA, but first I had to take a reality check. I did not have the tuition fee. I'd have to find thousands of US dollars. I would need someone to co-finance my stay.

I turned to my extended family.

In the meantime, Marsha was preparing the way for me to migrate. She and I are Campionites and have been friends since first form. She helped me apply to Howard and used her own money to pay the application fee. The only thing I did was to affix my signature to the document. That done, she submitted the application for me.

My application was successful, but now I had to make plans about how to finance my studies. Some of the members of my family came together and pooled their funds to cover the cost of my tuition. Other family members, on the other hand, for reasons best known to them, discouraged me from leaving. "Why you leaving your mother?" they said. "Don't go anywhere."

One of my relatives who was in the USA at the time became my greatest supporter. "Yes, come up," he said. "I will cosign a loan for you." This loan would cover the cost of my tuition and other expenses, so I wouldn't have to rely on those resources that my family had pooled to help me. He was a favorite relative and had been good to me, so when he went out on that limb to facilitate my studies in the USA, I was beyond grateful.

I'd saved as much as possible from the salary that I'd earned during my internship. This saving amounted to US$1,550. Throughout the application process, I had to send documents by Federal Express to Howard. After paying the cost for sending those documents, I was left with a little over US$1,300. I bought my plane ticket at the last minute, so it was expensive. My uncle, Delroy, gave me half of the cost of the ticket, and I found the rest. After all was said and done, I was left with US$900, which I'd leave for the States with and a promise of more from a relative. This was not the strongest financial limb to hold on to, but it was all I had, and I clung to it. My options were clear. Either I stayed in Jamaica and be satisfied with a mediocre salary, have a passel of kids, be beholden to somebody, and become my mom. Or I could just leave and be the person my mom expected me to be.

I was confident that once I got to the US, I would find the "better" I was looking for through my hard work—which I intended to put in so that I could take care of her. At that point I was driven by the need to take care of both her and my brother. I wanted to make sure that I changed the narrative about my family—a narrative of struggle.

I've always had very high expectations of myself. I knew that I couldn't become the president of the United States of America, but I knew that if someone gave me the opportunity to leave Jamaica—gave me the resources so that I could have even the slightest chance of becoming successful, I was going to take it and make use of it. I'd seen people who had gone to the USA drastically improve their lives because of the opportunities that they found there. Those opportunities beckoned me.

When I left Jamaica for Howard University, I wasn't just going there to make a better life for myself and my mother and brother. I was also running. Running from my life as I knew it—the constant cycle of mental anguish and the nagging belief that I had that if I stayed, I would not realize my full potential. But there were other small annoyances that nagged at me. I had unfinished business, and I was not going to rest easy until I had completed it.

That unfinished business was to prove my naysayers wrong.

I left Jamaica to prove to my primary school teacher that I wasn't the failure that she had predicted and gossiped about.

I left Jamaica to prove to the community that traumatized me—because I was fatherless and poor—that I was worth something. People in my community expected that by the age of twenty, I would have had several children, all fatherless like me. They did not expect me to be successful at all. And I wanted to show the moms who'd shunned me, who did not want me to be better off than their children and didn't expect much of me, that I didn't choose to be fatherless or impoverished, and I wasn't the failure that they had predicted. That I was worth more than the rumors they'd helped to propagate about me.

I was running away from the people who hurt me and preyed upon me, to prove to them that their predatory behaviors toward me would not stop me from believing in my worth. That they would not stop me from continuing to strive for what I wanted out of life, and thriving while doing so.

I also left Jamaica to mend a broken heart. My boyfriend and I had split for the second time. I was devastated and wanted to prove to him that he had done a dumb thing. I had to leave Jamaica because if I'd stayed, I didn't think I could show him what I was capable of and make him realize the huge mistake he'd made when he discontinued our relationship. And this is one of the saddest things about me. All my life, I have been trying to prove to people how good I am—a self-imposed duty which is my motivation to keep on striving.

But more than anything, I left Jamaica to find me.

When I left my mom was ailing. She'd been diagnosed with breast cancer and had done a mastectomy, three days before I flew out. I went to Howard University to find information about this disease. I couldn't envision a life without her, and my spirituality convinced me that I was created to give God the glory, but I was created to serve my mom also. She'd spent her life making sacrifices for me. It was my time to give back to her.

When I left Jamaica, it was my first time flying. It was scary but liberating. I left Jamaica without even confirming who would pick me up at the Washington Reagan Airport. But there was no turning back now.

CHAPTER 11
THE ROSSERS

FRUIT TART

This is a rich, decadent dessert that reminds me of the life to which the Rossers introduced me. And this is Aunt Meg's (Dr. Neita-Rosser's) favorite dessert.

Ingredients for the crust

1 1/3 cup all-purpose flour

1/4 cup granulated sugar

1/2 tsp kosher salt

10 tbsp melted butter

1/2 tsp almond extract/vanilla

Ingredients for the filling

1/2 cup heavy cream

1 8-oz container mascarpone cheese

4 oz cream cheese, softened

1/2 cup powdered sugar

Juice of 1/2 lemon

1/2 tsp almond extract/vanilla

For the topping

1 cup strawberries, halved or diced

1 cup blackberries

1 cup raspberries

2 mandarins (mangarines in Jamaica)

1/3 cup blueberries

1/4 cup apricot preserves

Note: You may use whatever fruit you have at hand.

Preheat oven to 350°

To make crust:

In a large bowl, whisk together flour, sugar, and salt. Add melted butter and almond/vanilla extract and stir until dough forms. Press mixture into a 10" tart pan with a removable bottom, pressing dough all the way up the sides and until dough is smooth.

Prick crust all over with a fork and bake until golden, 20 to 25 minutes. Let crust cool completely.

Make filling: In a medium bowl, using a hand mixer, beat heavy cream until stiff peaks form. In a large bowl, beat mascarpone and cream cheese until smooth. Add powdered sugar, lemon juice, and almond/vanilla extract and beat until smooth. Fold in whipped cream.

Spread filling over cooled crust and arrange fresh fruit on top.

Heat preserves and 2 tsp water until warm. Glaze tart with mixture. Refrigerate tart until well chilled, at least 2 hours.

When I landed at the Reagan International Airport in Washington, D.C., two of my former classmates from Campion College were there waiting for me. Boy, was I relieved to see them! We went straight to the YARD of Howard University, where even more Campion and UTech colleagues welcomed and embraced me.

A few years ago I visited Howard University with my children, the lawn was still lush and the Howard quadrangle aka The Yard was just as busy as I had remembered it. Photo Credit: Dr. Oladi Bentho

When I entered the YARD, it was filled with students. The campus had a beautiful, well-manicured green lawn. Students were picnicking and playing football. They were happy, and it was infectious.

One thing that particularly stood out was the various groups having fun, dancing, singing and stepping. Howard University is the Mecca and is the birthplace of fraternities and sororities (the black Greek letter organizations) known as the Divine Nine. I remember seeing members of sororities and fraternities prancing and dancing around, and the freedoms and joys of youth on display in the yard consumed me. I had immediately begun to experience the rich legacy of HBCUs, and instinctively I understood this to be the immediate spirit of community my soul had been longing for. It suddenly dawned on me that I was saved. I was free! I felt lighter than I'd ever felt before. I was floating.

Memories of that day, August 18, 2001, often bring me to tears, because my life changed in that instant. I was in a new space, a different space, and I was happy. It was my redo. It was such a beautiful, sunny day! The day seemed somehow longer, filled with so much promise, so much endless possibilities!

After reaching the university, I called the relative who'd pledged to help access funding for my studies. I called and called, but there was no answer. I was a bit worried, but I left my things in Marsha's room and went about getting settled at Howard. I would call again later.

Before I left Marsha's room, Yinka, another Campionite, and I had a conversation that set me on the right track. I'd planned to do a biology major as a precursor to entering the medical school at Howard. As Yinka and I spoke, she advised me to change my Biology major and to transfer my UTech credits to the Clinical Laboratory Science Program. This would shorten the time it would take to complete the degree from four years to two. If I did a degree in my current field, she reasoned, I wouldn't have to worry about getting a job when I graduated.

I thought it was great advice, so I listened to her. We'd been schoolmates, after all, and so I knew that she would not lead me down the wrong path.

That same day, I went searching for Howard's equivalent of the UTech Medical Technology Department. After being pointed in the right direction, I found the Clinical Laboratory Sciences Department. At the time, an elderly Indian gentleman was the dean of that program. He looked at my transcript and said, "We've taken a lot of UTech students, so we know how advanced they are." He seemed happy that I was coming from UTech.

I said, "Wow. Really?" I was surprised. The administrators at Howard knew the UTech curriculum! They knew how successful the students could be in their program! That knowledge excited me. I was ready to start the program to show them that I could be successful too. Instantly, I was transferred in, and within thirty minutes, I was no longer a Biology major but a Clinical Lab Sciences major.

So, here I was at Howard University with no tuition fees and nowhere to sleep, because the funding that my relative had promised had not come through as yet. After completing my registration, the Dean of the Clinical Lab program said, "We even have a Jamaican on staff." I was curious, and happy, that a Jamaican was teaching at this prestigious university that I intended to attend.

When I was introduced, I realized that the Jamaican who was a member of staff was the deputy dean of the program, Dr. Marguerite Neita-Rosser and would be my teacher of Immunology. Later, I learned that she is from the prominent Neita family in Jamaica, and her sister with whom she shares a strong resemblance is Valerie Neita, that well-known Jamaican lawyer. I also learned that her nephews were Campionites.

After we had completed the getting-to-know-you phase of our relationship, the first question she asked me was, "So Altreisha, where are you staying?"

I told her that I was staying with my friend, Marsha, on the dorm by the Towers. I went on to tell her that I'd been trying to get in touch with my relative who had promised to co-sign my student loan, so that I could get housing on the dorm and start my classes, but that I couldn't reach him since I'd been there. I'd been trying but he was no longer answering his phone. She invited me to her office, and we started talking, and I told her everything about my desperate situation.

After listening to my story, she said, "Altreisha, would you like to come stay with Rufus and me?"

I wasn't sure that I'd heard her correctly. That offer had seemed too good to be true. Was it possible that I was being given a lifeline by someone I'd only just met?

Shock rendered me mute.

Remaining calm and dignified, she repeated the question. "Would you like to stay with Rufus and me until you figure out this tuition business?"

"Yes! Yes!" I quickly said, breaking out of my silence. I was not going to refuse. How could I? I had no choice. I was in America, homeless and broke. My relative had let me down. I'd believed in him, sure that he would have come through for me. But he hadn't, and now I was stranded. And just as He always does, God had sent angels in the form of the Rossers to rescue me.

Dr. Neita's offer was not too good to be true. It was in fact good, and it was true. She took me into her home where I lived for one year. The Rossers had two grown-up daughters, one who was in the military at the time, and another who was away at college. I was offered one of the vacant bedrooms. That was one problem solved for me. I did not have to worry about housing.

Funnily enough, I did not meet her husband for a long time because of his busy schedule. One day Dr. Neita-Rosser laughingly said, "I know you're probably thinking I don't have a husband, but I do, and I promise you'll meet him." And I eventually did meet him. He was a Pediatrician, who is very quiet, but super friendly.

But Dr. Neita-Rosser did so much more than provide a roof over my head. She advocated for me to get half of my tuition paid on entering Howard. Because of her advocacy, I got money to start my classes. You see, during my time at Howard incoming transfer students were not eligible for scholarships, but Mrs. Mounsey, the dean of the college at the time, saw me and made a way.

The Rosser household was warm. They took care of me, teaching me so much about life in America and about the finer things of life, taking up from where the McLeod's had left off. I remember one day I went with Dr. Neita and the family to a restaurant for breakfast, and I ordered home fries. I thought I'd ordered regular French fries, but I was wrong. Something was delivered to the table, but it was not the fries I had ordered so I continued waiting on my order. Nonchalantly, I turned to her and said, "My fries aren't here yet."

She said gently, "No, baby, these are what they call home fries." Talk about culture shock! In terms of being cultured and such, she really helped me.

She always told me, "Just be kind, Altreisha; kindness takes you far." I lived their kindness, and I prospered because of it. Their kindness has taken me a long way. From them I really understood the importance of giving without asking for something in return.

You don't know whose life you're changing when you give. Just give without questioning the circumstances of the person who is in need. Dr. Neita and the Rosser family gave to me, having only met me that day—someone who didn't talk much about herself. Yet they had seen it fit to take me in. I've become such a giver because of the example of my mom, the McLeods and the Rossers.

I owe the Rossers much. Without the intervention of Dr Neita-Rosser, I don't know what would have happened to me in the USA. I might possibly have had to defer my studies and scrounge around in the country until I had regularized my status. The Rossers were my guardian angels at Howard, and I continue to be grateful to them for their generosity and love.

CHAPTER 12
HOWARD UNIVERSITY

CHOCOLATE MOLTEN LAVA CAKE

This is one of my favorite desserts. It is soft, with tender crumbs and all that chocolate goodness whooshing out. It reflects my state of contentment at Howard and in the knowledge that I and the many shades of empowered Caribbean and African-American students who populated the university were on our way to making our mark in our fields of study. We were moving towards our destiny.

Ingredients

4 oz semi-sweet chocolate chips or baking chocolate

½ cup unsalted butter

1 cup icing sugar

2 eggs

2 egg yolks

3 oz flour

Instructions

Preheat oven to 425° F.

Grease 4 small ramekin dishes with grease of your choice and arrange them on a baking sheet.

Combine butter and chocolate in a pan over low heat until melted. Carefully heat so as not to burn the ingredients.

Mix in the icing sugar until it is fully incorporated into the chocolate butter mixture.

Add eggs and egg yolks and beat into the mixture.

Gently fold in flour until combined.

Pour the batter into the ramekin dishes until ¾ full.

Bake in the preheated oven for at 425°F for 12-13 minutes. Check baking progress after 10 minutes. Edges should be firm, and center should be a tad soft.

Cool for a few minutes then gently use a knife to pull the cake away from the edges, then invert onto plate.

Serve with whatever ingredient you like, whether strawberries, a dusting of icing sugar, vanilla ice cream…

Best if served immediately.

I'd migrated only three weeks before the September 11, 2011 terrorist attack on the Twin Towers in New York. Seeing the smoke billowing from buildings on television shocked and scared me. That event shook my faith in my decision to study in the US. I wanted to return home, but to what? The answer to that question sobered me.

Being in the States seemed, to me, to be a thousand times better than being back in Jamaica and just enduring as I had been doing there—enduring poverty, enduring the frustrations of not being able to realize my potential, enduring my inability to help my mother in her illness, enduring the frustration of that broken relationship, enduring the hopelessness that had been in front of me as far as the eyes could see. So, like the rest of the population in America, I weathered that storm.

I had known about Howard University because several Campionites had matriculated there after sixth form. Also, I'd known that it is a prestigious private university in Washington, D.C. that had a significant focus on research and a large black student population. That information had not swayed my decision to attend one way or the other. My primary aim was to go somewhere where I had the opportunity to better my condition in life. Any university in the USA would have been all right for me, but Howard seemed to have chosen me when my friend decided to send in an application for me.

I was there to do another undergraduate degree, majoring in Biology, having already received an undergraduate Diploma in Medical Technology from the University of Technology in Jamaica. And because of my mom's cancer diagnosis, I was focused on finding out as much as I could about the disease, and eventually doing medical research to be able to support her with information in her quest for a cure.

I completed my Bachelor of Science degree in Clinical Laboratory Sciences in two years. I did a minimum of 20 credits per semester, and I still achieved a GPA of 4.0. I understood that my GPA was the currency that was going to pay my tuition. I didn't have any money coming in from anywhere, and I knew that anything over a GPA of 3.8 was guaranteed money. So, I was just doing the damn thing, and I was getting my tuition paid.

Meanwhile, Howard University not only embraced me, but changed me, as well. I received several scholarships so that I could afford my education, and in return I was top of the class, until I completed the course and ultimately graduated summa cum laude with a near perfect GPA. When Howard gave me all that money to finance my studies, I thought, *Yes! This is the chance I've been waiting on, and I'm going to grab this opportunity and live up to my name, Altreisha.*

And I did. I excelled from day one at the University and continued to excel in all of my courses, graduating with the highest honor for my undergraduate degree.

After I completed my bachelor's degree, I transitioned directly into the doctoral program at Howard University Medical School in the Department of Microbiology and completed that degree in five years. They believed, rightly, that I had the intelligence to manage the rigors of the study that a doctorate degree demanded—my undergraduate degree had proven that. Howard University believed in me when all I had was US$900. They deviated from the norm to give an impoverished girl like me a scholarship to begin classes, and within six years I'd exponentially changed my socioeconomic status.

In the Department of Microbiology, students could specialize in any of the following options: Molecular Biology, Virology, Immunology, or Mycology. I chose Virology because I wanted to find out if there was a link between viruses and cancer. I wanted to study the oncological properties of viruses and to ultimately develop relevant therapeutics and vaccines.

I'd shown myself, my professors at Howard and everyone else that I could achieve much. I was satisfied with my achievements. When I was born, my mom had placed all her hopes and dreams in me, and I had to live up to those expectations, because I believed in her dream for my life. I wanted to make something of myself. I'd come to the USA, thinking that I was going to get my degrees, I was going to get married, and I was going to have all the happiness in the world—those were my expectations for my life. And I surpassed all my expectations.

At Howard I built on the confidence I'd been developing in Jamaica, and I actualized my potential. I only needed to do well to be able to change my mother's life and mine. My self-belief blossomed. The brokenness that had lived inside me was healing. I'd found myself in a new country and a new city where nobody had any preconceived ideas about who I was. No one knew me, and no one made assumptions. I found friends who nurtured me. But I was protective of who I was, continuing to hide myself from the past, because it was that space that had hurt me.

After I finished Howard with a doctorate in Virology—Oncology and Virology focus—I worked as a vaccine scientist before returning to university, this time George Washington University, to do a master's in Public Health. In this degree, I focused on health disparities and the impact of infectious diseases on the vulnerable. I wanted to strengthen and solidify my infectious disease chops, as I was getting ready to start my consulting firm doing work around vaccine sciences and viruses. I was trying to make myself a well-rounded individual.

My formal education in the USA was completed within a little over a decade of my being there. That education propelled me to opportunities that I couldn't have dreamed of when I was in Jamaica. Even though I felt that I was destined to do great things, and I wanted to do great things, I couldn't see clearly what those great things were. Howard University clarified for me what I was capable of by opening countless doors for me through the education that it gave me. I've walked through those doors and will continue to walk through others as they open to me, thanks to the impetus that the education at Howard gave me.

CHAPTER 13
FRIENDSHIPS

This dessert is time-consuming to make but wonderful to eat. It involves different levels of effort, and the final product has different layers of flavors that capture the essence of the friendships that have blessed my life.

Danish

Prep Time: 50 mins

Bake Time: 16 to 18 mins

Ingredients

Dough

454 grams unsalted butter, at room temperature (softened not melted)

5 1/2 cups or 660 grams all-purpose flour

1/3 cup (67g) granulated sugar

4 tsp instant yeast

2 1/2 tsp (15g) salt (if you use salted butter, reduce salt to 1 1/2 tsps or 9 grams of salt

1/2 to 1 tsp cardamom for traditional flavor (optional)

1 tsp vanilla extract

1 cup (227g) cold milk

1/3 to 1/2 cup (76g to 113g) lukewarm water

2 large eggs

Cheese filling

4 oz or 56.5 grams cream cheese

1/2 cup (113g) cottage cheese or ricotta cheese

3 tbsp (35g) granulated sugar

1 large egg

1/4 tsp salt

Fruit filling

About 1 to 1 1/4 cups (298g to 369g) jam, preserves, or canned fruit pie filling

Topping

1 large egg white and 1 tbsp cold water beaten lightly

Glaze

1 1/2 cups (170g) confectioners' sugar or glazing sugar

2 to 2 1/2 tbsp (28g to 35g) water or milk, enough to make a thin glaze that can be drizzled over the danish

Pinch of salt

Crushed nuts, optional; to garnish

Instructions

Begin by cutting off 2 tbsp of the butter for the recipe.

In a large bowl, whisk together all the dry ingredients (the flour, sugar, yeast, salt, and cardamom). Add the 2 tbsp of cold butter, working it in with your fingers until no large lumps remain.

Add the vanilla, milk, water, and eggs to the dry ingredients. Mix and knead to make a cohesive, but quite sticky dough. You may use a bread machine set on the dough cycle or you may use a mixer. If you use a mixer, you will need a spatula to clean down the sides of the bowl to incorporate all the mixture into the dough.

Scrape the dough into a ball and transfer it to a floured work surface. Cover it with plastic wrap, and let it rest for 10 minutes.

Divide butter in half. Put each piece of butter on a floured parchment or plastic wrap. Coat the butter with a thin layer of flour. Pound butter until flattened and shape into a rectangle of 6" x 9". You should have two 6" x 9" rectangular pieces of butter. Keep them cool by placing in the refrigerator while you work.

Roll the dough into a rectangle approximately 12" wide and 24" long.

Place one of the butter pieces onto the center third of the dough. Fold one side over the butter to cover it. Place the other butter piece atop the folded-over dough and fold the remaining dough up over it. Pinch the sides closed.

Turn the 12" side to you. Roll the dough into a 10" x 24" rectangle. Fold each side into the center; then fold one side over the other to make a rectangular packet about 6" x 10".

Dust the surface of the dough with flour, wrap it in plastic wrap, and chill in the refrigerator for about 20 minutes.

Remove the dough from the fridge, and again roll it into a rectangle, about 10" x 24". Fold it into a packet of about 7" x 12" by folding each side into the center; then fold one side over the other to make a rectangle.

Roll one final time, fold into a packet, and flour the dough lightly. Wrap loosely in plastic and chill it for at least 2 hours but up to 24 hours.

Select your fillings then shape the pastries. You may add both fillings in one pastry or you may use different fillings in the pastries.

Make the cheese filling by combining all the ingredients until you get a smooth mass.

Remove the dough from the refrigerator when you are ready to make your pastries, unwrap it, and cut off a third of it. Return the remainder to the fridge.

Divide the third of the dough that you cut off into 12 pieces. Roll each into a smooth ball, then flatten the balls into 3" to 3 1/2" rounds. Make the center thinner than the edges, so that the filling will have somewhere to lodge. Place the rounds on a baking sheet that is lined with parchment or one that is greased and dusted with flour.

Repeat the process with the remaining dough.

Cover the danish lightly with greased plastic wrap and let them rise for about 1 hour. Ten minutes before the hour is up, preheat the oven to 400°F.

Use your fingers to create a well in the center of the dough and a tsp or so of the filling into the well of each round.

Brush the exposed edges of pastry with the egg wash.

Bake the pastries for 15 to 18 minutes, until they're golden brown. Remove them from the oven, and transfer to a cooling rack. Glaze while hot or after they have cooled.

Drizzle the glaze atop the pastries. You may sprinkle with crush nuts.

We humans are social beings. Most of us need to be a part of a group to make us feel as though we belong, to make us feel important, to make us feel that our contributions to the group are important, whatever that group is. There is a web of social relationships that we enter to feel a connection to each other and to something bigger than ourselves.

I am no Sociologist, but I think that churches were so packed when I was growing up in Golden River, because people craved that connection with each other and that connection to a power greater than themselves. Even though we had our familial groups that extended over several generations and served several purposes—providing companionship for its members and being a refuge from all the bad things that could happen outside of the home— we needed other connections in our lives, a web of social networks.

All the groups to which humans belong meet several of the needs that we have, according to Maslow, that eminent psychologist—the need for safety, the need for belonging and love, and the need for esteem. These needs motivate us to keep on going, in spite of the challenges in our lives.

Our friendship groups are important in our lives. They are made up of mostly of our peers with whom we socialize to find validation for our actions as humans who matter. Some friends are closer than some, but they validate us and make us feel good about ourselves.

I'd had a few friends in Golden River, and I made a few more after I left. Some have taught me that I do not quite understand the meaning of friendship. I believe that if you are my friend we can confide in each other, especially about inconsequential things— things that everybody will soon know about, things that are good in your life. I have these friends and I've had others who did not think it was important to share some things with friends.

The Campion College connection

I made some friends at Campion College who are still my friends today. And there is even one girl who was there with whom I didn't get along, but she is now my good friend. Some of the friends I made at Campion deserve special mention. Sekeywi, Janine, Crystal,

Simone, Geli and Marsha hold special places in my heart. Marsha is the one who helped me get to Howard.

Even though they are all my friends, Sekeywi and I shared a special bond. Of all the people I met at Campion College, she was different. She was caring and down to earth and she has not changed since then. Even though my house was not much and was cramped for space, as a "rich girl," she didn't mind staying there. She came. She stayed. She did not judge. Mom would welcome her when she visited. I was also similarly welcomed at her parents' house.

Janine lived in my community. We would take the bus together. She was one of those people with whom I shared a lot of laughs. We lost contact for a long time, then we regained the connection in time for my wedding in 2011.

Then there is my friend Josina and her dad, DK. She and I were very close until we changed shifts and majors in fourth and fifth forms. Her dad, Mr. Duncan, was fun and Josina was just like him. He took care of us when I visited them. I was safe.

Moira is special to me. We never got along in high school, mind you, but we became fast friends when both of us met in sixth form at Queen's. I was so happy to see her face that first day in sixth form, and I was happy for the opportunity for that do over with her, that I grabbed it. I guess distance and life experiences change one's perspectives about things. We both ended up at Howard.

Karla is the glue that keeps our class together. She is that Campionite you love to see and who loves to see you. The Class of 1995 does epitomize the strength of the red—our school color. We've become a very close group.

The classes of 1994, 1995 and 1996 have embraced me. They cheer me on. They lift me up. They celebrate me. Now that I am older and have better experiences in my life than the ones I had when I was at Campion, I sometimes wonder if I'd projected my insecurities onto my peers and had shut them out of my life while I was at school. They were only children living in their truth, while I was living in mine—truths that didn't intersect at that time.

The Campion College connection is still alive and well today, but I must say that it was after I moved on from there that I truly found myself.

The Queen's connection

Although I made friends and acquaintances at Campion, it was when I went to Queen's that I made friends who truly understood me. At Queen's, these people cared about me, believed that I mattered, and told and showed me that I mattered. Queen's was a good space for me and represented my happy high school years. I loved it there, and I miss those girls, and the black girl joy that came with them. Maybe, I was more open because my confidence had started growing, and my heart was healing, and I was finding my own black girl joy in myself.

I made lifelong friends at The Queen's School, as well; three of whom have since passed. I still have these friends because they are genuine and because my socioeconomic situation hadn't been a prerequisite for our friendship. Money and status did not matter to those girls. I was just Altreisha to them. I felt at home there. That may be because there was a mixture of students from all socioeconomic status attending the school who integrated well with each other, but Queen's was my place.

I was a part of a group of girls at Queen's called the Ackee Tree Crew. We were a group of teenagers from various socioeconomic strata. We coined our name from the fact that during our breaks, we would hang out under the ackee tree in the schoolyard and talk about whatever interested any of us.

It was at Queen's that I became best friends with Tremone. I confided in her, but not a lot. It is not my nature to say too much about myself and the circumstances of my life. She confided in me, and I have never shared her secrets. Once I'm your friend, I'm your ride or die, so I will take your secrets with me to the grave.

By the time I went to Queen's, I'd begun to find myself, so I understood who I wanted to be my friends. I knew the types of friendships I wanted. I knew what I would accept and what I wouldn't. I knew my worth and the kind of friendship I could give to someone. If someone didn't value who I was as a friend, then screw them! Today, those girls from Queen's and I are all still friends.

The UTech connection

In spite of my challenges while at UTech, my experience there was pivotal in helping to pull me back from the brink of disaster. Sometimes, I thought about the seeming hopelessness of my situation and wondered if life was worth living like that. Most times, I believed it wasn't. But the friends I met there—Damiso, Oneka, Trudy, Kahlilia, Keasha, Kurt, Keilia, Sly, Walworth and Tre—helped me to change my perspective. They too have become lifelong friends. My life was spared because they forced me to choose my life. They chose to do life with me, and when I couldn't stand or breathe, they held me up and resuscitated me each time I flatlined. My life mattered to them, and their lives mattered to me.

Even though I made these lifelong friends at Campion, at Queen's and at UTech, and we've been through many good and bad times, and I value these friendships, I did not show them all of myself over the years of our friendship. No one knew much about me, except what I chose to share. Tremone, Marsha and my friend "Kiwi" knew more about me than most.

The Spanish Town connection

When I lived in Ensom City, Spanish Town, I had a close friend. We traveled to school in Kingston, and when we graduated high school, we traveled to different colleges in Kingston. One day she simply stopped going to school. I was worried. I asked her why she'd stopped. She just shrugged every time I asked. By that time my friend had been out of college for a few months. I asked a relative of hers if she was okay. The relative said she was fine.

Little did I know that the family was getting ready to migrate. She gave me the news two days before their departure. That was a dagger in my heart, because I thought we'd been friends, and her migrating was not such a big deal that she couldn't have shared it with me. I'd have been happy for her if she'd told me in the beginning, as I was happy for her when she eventually told me.

Some Jamaicans are like this. When big events, like migration, a job interview or even an exam, are about to happen in their lives, they will not share the details of these events with anyone but their closest family. They will wait until the last minute to divulge any details to anyone for fear that someone may put a stumbling block in their way to prevent them from achieving their goal.

I don't think my friend thought I posed any danger to her family's plan—at least I hope she didn't—but I was kept out of the loop, and that bothered me. I now get it, but her action still makes me feel sidelined, all these years later. These actions were not novel to me. I'd gotten so used to being undermined, looked down on, talked about and frowned upon by some of my friends, that I just accepted whatever came my way, remaining laser-focused on thinking on better eventually coming.

Having thought about the action of this friend though, of keeping her impending migration from me, I wondered if she too was not doing exactly what I was doing—hiding some of herself from the world. Her reasons for doing that were different than mine, but she was entitled to her privacy as I was to mine. If I'd thought about this side of the issue, I might not have been so hurt. But as they say, wisdom comes with age. It sure does, at least for me.

My first boyfriend

One summer I met a boy in Mother's in York Plaza, Half-Way-Tree. He was a friend of a friend with whom I was there to have lunch. She'd invited me there to meet him and another friend. I was sixteen and I'd just completed Campion and waiting on my CXC exam results.

That boy and I did not get along when we first met. He and his friend were a little immature, I thought, and I found them annoying. I decided to leave. I thought I was wasting my time, and I did not have any time for time-wasting or time-wasters. By then I had begun to develop a low tolerance for such people. Once people started to annoy me, I had no qualms about getting up and leaving. That was what I did. I took my things, jumped over his legs, walked to the bus stop and took my bus back to Spanish Town.

I guess this boy could not understand my indifference, so he got my number from my friend and called me. We started chatting and found that we had common interests. We were friends for a long time.

He took the time to get to know me. I appreciated that. I discovered that I mattered to him, and he showed me that I did. But better still, had no qualms telling and showing others, even his parents, that I was someone who mattered.

His parents are decent human beings. Whenever I visited their son at home, they made sure that I got home safely. They would check to see if I made it home. They cared about me, someone else's child. This is evidence of the good qualities they possess, and they passed on these qualities to their son, who is a decent human being as well.

His baby sister was also the warmest little girl you would ever meet. Every time I visited, she would run and embrace my legs, squealing my name as she did so. I loved hugging on that little girl. Her love was contagious. I saw love in all the members of that family, and I learned how to love from them. That whole family made me feel so loved. Their love was a balm for my bruised heart.

That boy would tell me that I was smart and beautiful. He was someone who would make time to listen to me. If he heard people saying bad things about me, he would protect me. He never repeated what he heard, preferring to walk around being angry all day. Such a weight he'd carry around for me. He'd give me advice, though, such as: "Be careful of…" He told me to ignore the things that some people were saying, because I knew the truth about myself, and he knew the truth about me. Imagine that!

After he came into my life, I could feel my confidence growing. I was unstoppable, because he taught me my self-worth. Nobody could say anything bad about me when he was around, because he was going to defend me. He helped me change the way I saw myself. He loved me, respected me and he believed in me.

He, only sixteen himself, taught me that I was worthy. He had such high expectations of me, but it was difficult to believe it myself. *Why did he choose me?* I'd often ask myself. Slowly, our young love did its transformative work on me and made me believe that I was actually lovable, that I was important to someone else.

When I was eighteen, he broke up with me just before he started attending the University of the West Indies (UWI). He started dating girls at his university. I thought he had broken up with me, because he'd found girls who were better than me. That shook me for a while.

At the same time, all that confidence that he had helped instill in me was still there. It then became my goal to prove to him that he had missed out, that whomever he had chosen over me was definitely not better than me. I was right, because we began dating again at UTech, before we broke up for good.

Years later we spoke about our relationship. He told me that there was so much that I'd needed then, and there was so much that he'd needed for himself that he did not think he could have given me what I needed and become what he wanted to be, as well. I was surprised that at eighteen he'd been capable of that level of maturity of thought.

He told me that it was not that he'd rejected me, but he'd seen so much greatness in me that he hadn't wanted to stand in my way of achieving it. Besides, he'd needed to find his own greatness. I thought that was cool.

He always told me how driven I was to prove my greatness. He said I was my greatest critic. If I were not given the chance to be all that I could be, I wouldn't have been satisfied. He didn't want to stand in my way because I needed me to be okay with me. I don't know if he was gaslighting me, but I believed him.

I don't know that at sixteen or eighteen he could have seen that and was only better able to articulate those sentiments now that he had matured. Or probably he'd come to those revelations in hindsight. Whatever had brought it on, I appreciated him for saying it. I think, as he grew older, he'd realized that he needed to achieve things for himself, and I needed to achieve things on my own. To my mind that's love.

So even though we'd parted years ago, he was still showing me now that I mattered by trying to put his thoughts on our past relationship into words. By doing that, he helped me to put that relationship into perspective as well. Now, I am successful in his eyes, and he is successful in mine. That matters to me. I've achieved my dreams and he has achieved his. That's something to celebrate.

He was that one constant friend who kept building me up and made me feel that I was worthy of something. He was a light that guided me out of the dark place in my life that threatened to overwhelm me. He was one of my guardian angels who was sent to me at a pivotal point in my life, when I desperately needed to be understood. And he gave me the space to be vulnerable by giving me his attention and forcing me to count my blessings instead of what I deemed to be my afflictions.

Even now, he has no idea how much he still means to me and how grateful I am for his friendship. Having been a part of my life and helping me to cultivate a positive perception of myself, I credit him for having given me the confidence to keep on going amid the worst difficulties of my life. He is a light from my past.

There are other friends whom I've met in other spheres of my life who I haven't mentioned here, but they are equally significant to my life. All my friends have been rocks to me over the years. Each of them has contributed something that has improved my life in some way. I'm grateful to them for all the lessons they've taught me. I've learned from them and have been using them to strengthen my relationships in the social networks in which I find myself today.

CHAPTER 14
TRAUMA

LEMON MERINGUE PIE

This dessert is so attractive to look at! It's tart, creamy and sweet all at the same time with a flaky crust and a soft core. It has to be prepared with care to get the right consistency and must be stored with care to prevent it from losing its consistency after it comes out of the oven. I needed to be nurtured and handled with care by some of the people I met during much of my formative years to be my best self, just as this dessert needs to be created and handled with care to be its best.

Ingredients

1 9-inch pie crust (store bought or homemade)

1 cup granulated sugar

2 tbsp all-purpose flour

3 tbsp cornstarch

1/4 tsp salt

1 1/2 cups water

1/2 cup lemon juice

1 tbsp lemon zest

2 tbsp unsalted butter

4 large egg yolks, beaten

The meringue

1 tbsp cornstarch

1/3 cup water

1/4 tsp cream of tartar

1/3 cup granulated sugar

4 large egg whites at room temperature

Instructions

For the Lemon Filling:

Separate egg yolks from the egg whites and set aside both.

In a medium saucepan, whisk together 1 cup sugar, flour, cornstarch, and salt. Stir in water, lemon juice and lemon zest.

Cook over medium-high heat, stirring frequently, until mixture comes to a boil. Remove from heat and stir in butter.

In a small bowl, beat the egg yolks. Add a spoonful of the hot sugar mixture into the egg yolk mixture and whisk together. We don't want the mixture to curdle, so we add a spoonful of the hot mixture at a time to temper the mixture.

Whisk the egg yolk mixture back into remaining sugar mixture in the pot.

Bring to a boil and continue to cook while stirring constantly, until thick. Remove from heat. Pour filling into baked pie shell.

Preheat oven to 350° F.

For the meringue

In a small saucepan, whisk together cornstarch and water.

Cook over medium heat, stirring constantly as the mixture thickens, until it begins to simmer. Remove from heat and set aside.

In a small bowl stir together cream of tartar and sugar. In a large bowl beat the egg whites with electric mixers until frothy.

With the mixtures running, add the sugar, a spoonful at a time, until fully incorporated. Continue beating until soft peaks appear.

Add the cornstarch mixture while beating, a spoonful at a time. Mix until stiff peaks form, about 1-2 minutes.

Pour the meringue onto the hot lemon filling in the pie shell. Spoon the meringue around the edge of the pie first, and then add spoonfuls to the center until the entire surface is covered.

Make sure the meringue is touching the outer pie crust so that it doesn't shrink away while baking. Use the back of your spoon to create decorative peaks in the meringue.

Bake in preheated oven for 10 minutes or until the meringue is lightly browned.

My mom told me that when I was a little girl—about two or three years old—I wasn't afraid to voice an opinion. If I saw somebody I thought was ugly, I would call them out on it, but I'd use my dress to cover my face after I had given them my home truth, because I probably couldn't bear looking at their ugliness, as I saw it in my toddler's eyes.

I can't remember any such thing, but every time I think about it, I say, "How rude!" At the same time, I'm curious to know what criteria I'd used to judge the ugliness of those people who might have been trying to be nice to me when I'd only paid them back with insults. Again, I don't know, because I have never been one to hurt someone deliberately.

It was rude of me then to call anyone ugly—that can be forgiven due to my age at that time. One glaring truth in doing so then was the fact that I had a voice, and I was not afraid to use it—though in the wrong way.

By the age of six, seven I'd lost my voice.

Looking back, I can't think of a specific incident that had caused that catastrophe in my life. It must have happened as a result of the shock of things someone, a relative much older than me, forced me to endure for her own amusement. How could she have done it, I've asked myself time and time again. This person had become my pimp, even though I had no desire to be pimped out.

I had little understanding of the world then, having lived a simple, sheltered life with people whom I was sure loved me, except for a few who would become the bane in my life throughout my childhood and in my adult years.

Why didn't I say something to my mother after the first incident? Better yet, why didn't I say no to the proposition and run away? I don't know.

Were there threats involved? I don't remember.

All I remember was feeling like dirt every summer when I had to reprise my role in that drama for an audience of one. However, things lost have a way of being found, and I did eventually find my voice again.

I'm from a huge family. My grandparents had eleven children and some of them had children. Every summer, most of the children would congregate at my grandparents' house for two months of fun and games. And I enjoyed those fun and games with my cousins. Among them was an older female relative, at whose hands some of the things I suffered were the stuff of which movies are made.

A male relative used to visit my grandparents' home for a few weeks over the summer holidays. He was a year younger than I. This older relative took pleasure in experimenting with our bodies. She would encourage him to take advantage of me while she watched, and he obeyed her. He seemed to have lost his voice just as I had lost mine.

Young as I was, there was a nagging voice at the back of my head saying, *This is wrong! This is wrong! This is wrong!* But I didn't know what to do about it. I just endured while tamping down my resentment. I'm still traumatized by that incident and often wonder if my cousin ever thinks about it. If he has, what has it done to his mental health, because it has certainly taken a toll on mine?

What this relative probably saw as harmless fun then, and after having enjoyed it had comfortably put it out of her mind, I saw as harmful fun—something that had caused my resentment against her to fester like a sore, and buried it deep in my mind, hoping never to resurrect it.

But I've had a change of mind.

It's a heavy, unnecessary weight that I have been forcing myself to carry over the years.

That relative was a test in my life that I had difficulty passing when I was younger. Today, I'm much older and wiser, but she is still a test I have not been able to pass. She's been traumatizing me all my life.

I remember when I was at Campion College, I used to have a diary in which I wrote some rich details of my future life. It was a manifesto of sorts for my life. I mapped out where I wanted to see myself and how I wanted to live. The life I'm living now.

I did not keep the diary in the room that my mom and I shared. Instead, I kept it in the room where all the children slept. One day, my mother's youngest sister found the diary and the key to open it. She read it without my knowledge and used my dreams to torment me.

One day out of the blue I heard her say, "So you rich, eh." She was laughing at me. She had read every word and shared the contents with everyone, violating my privacy. And there was nothing I could do about it.

This was yet another adult, a close relative, who believed that I couldn't achieve much. It's difficult to be neutral about her, even now, considering all the bad things she did to me when I was a child.

Then there was the boyfriend of my mother's younger sister who abused me. He was a short, burly, gentleman who was active in the church. A Christian, he called himself. He played several musical instruments. He also sang in the choir and thought he could sing, and by country people's standards, he probably could carry a note, but he was nothing but an infidel. He was a cheater who'd impregnated this relative while being committed to another. He had a good job and was one of the first persons in the community to possess a car. A big shot, he considered himself. That gentleman would fondle me when my mom was absent.

Again, I kept silent.

Knowing what I know now, if I had told my mom about that abuse back then, my older relative and that good Christian gentleman would have paid dearly for it. But I didn't tell. I bore the burden of that abuse alone. Why? It could be that I was too ashamed of what was happening to me to share that sordid story with anyone. So like everything bad that happened to me, I just packed it away at the back of my mind and tried to forget it, while I took advantage of the good that abounded around me—the good that my mother and my grandparents ensured that I got.

My excitement when I learned that we were leaving Golden River had nothing to do with the abuse I suffered, because I didn't quite understand what was being done to me until much later. So, I was not running away from that. I was running toward "better," but one of the nightmares that I was trying to forget traveled with me.

It was in Spanish Town that the sexual abuse by that male predator continued. That perverted Christian gentleman who had legitimized his relationship with my relative, by then, had tagged along with us to Spanish Town. When he got the opportunity—when we were alone at home, he would touch my breasts. I remember my shock when it happened again, this time in our new home.

It happened again and again and again.

And still I kept quiet.

After we settled in Spanish Town—everyone had moved there including my mother's youngest sister and her younger brothers—we lived in a three-bedroom house. My mother had one bedroom that she shared with my brother and me. My mother's younger sister had the other room, and the boys had the third room. That Christian guy was always in my aunt's room. Sometimes he would sit on her bed and play his guitar. I wasn't old enough to understand that they were in a relationship.

One thing I distinctly remember about him, though, is that he was a lecherous son of you know what. When the other adults had gone to work, or were out of the house, leaving us children alone, he plotted and always succeeded in getting me into his clutches. At our first house, he would send my brother and my youngest uncle across the road to the shop to buy cheese. I was the girl, so I wasn't expected to leave the house. Then he would start touching me. He was just in my clothes, fondling me, squeezing my nipples. He didn't say a word. I remember the sounds and smells that crept into the house as he violated me— the smell of parched peanuts being prepared by the peanut vendor who lived next door and the rattling of the grill when my relatives who were sent to the shop to buy cheese returned home. When he heard the sound of the grill being opened, he would stop. In Spanish Town, I endured the silent squeezing of my nipples, that constant violation of my person. It was just crazy, but I didn't know how to stop him.

Those episodes would happen in the afternoons after school. He used to work on shifts. When we got home, he would have already slept and getting ready to go to work on the night shift. That's how he ended up at the house. After work, he would come over because our house was closer than where he lived. My aunt was either going back to school or doing extra lessons, so she was not at home on weekdays when he was there.

The last time that man touched me, I was about ten and a half; my first term at Campion. I was in the living room napping on a sofa when I felt my nipples being squeezed. I jumped out of my sleep to see that wretched man bent over me and I lost it. In that moment, I found the strength to fight back. I was angry and tired of allowing him to violate me. I screamed at him to leave me the hell alone. I told him not to touch me again, and I said much more. He immediately backed off, embarrassed I'm sure that I'd blurted out his nasty secret. I'd had enough. Finally, I'd found my voice again, and had begun to learn its power.

But I did not tell my mom.

My mother's youngest sister had been in the kitchen when I was railing at that man. I'm pretty sure that she realized what I had been enduring at his hands all those years, but she held her tongue!

That man and my uncle were friends. In fact, it was my uncle who'd introduced him into our lives through our church in Golden River. Many years later when I told him that his friend had touched me, he was so angry. I felt that if he had gotten his hands on him then, he would have strangled him.

A broken relationship

My mother's younger sister and I had a good relationship over the years, in spite of her spouse who had caused me such trauma when I was a child. While I hated her man, I never hated her. There is much that I admire about her.

One of the first things I recognized about her, and which sets her apart from others, is her penmanship. It is beautiful. I spent hours trying to perfect my own by studying hers. I was successful, and I was complimented for it when I was in school. Without her modeling what great penmanship should look like, I might not have mastered it when I was younger.

Another commendable trait she possesses is her love for her sister—my mother. She would do anything for her. They are best friends. I appreciated her for that.

But her shining quality is her love for and belief in education. She has taken advantage of schooling up to the graduate level and encourages everyone she meets to do the same. Like many Jamaicans who'd endured poverty, she believes that education is the key to success.

Moreover, she was a rock to me when I first arrived in the US. She welcomed me, and I was glad about that. I was in Washington, D.C.

and she was in another state. She always welcomed my visits and would pack a "goodie" basket of food for me to take back to school every time I visited her. And I could call her up at any time and we would talk about anything. I thank her for the food and the listening ear that she gave me when I needed it.

A few years ago, I got into an argument with her about a domestic matter regarding my mom. She'd annoyed me. She'd refused to acknowledge my point of view and had been quite dismissive of my concerns regarding my mother and I don't tolerate anyone taking advantage of my mom! I wanted to bring her down a peg or two, so I called her a pedophile's wife. Some people may consider this childish and in poor taste—which it probably was—but I was livid. My blood was boiling and all the secondhand hurt and anger that I had bottled up and was carrying around over the years finally spilled out.

Instead of being shocked at the evil that her husband had perpetrated against me and commiserating with me, she dug her heels in and supported her husband. She said that I'd enjoyed the abuse, and I'd sat on her husband's lap for cheese—she made up some crazy stuff. She told me how she'd cleaned my shit when I was younger and how I was fatherless—*she actually threw that in my face*. She defended her man by calling me a liar and reiterated that I must have enjoyed her husband touching me.

I was shocked at her response and searched my mind for anyone who could have corroborated my story. Then I remembered my mom's youngest sister who'd been in the kitchen when I'd blasted that man. I told my mom that her youngest sister had witnessed the incident. When she asked her youngest sister about the incident, she corroborated my story. But when her sister, the wife of the pedophile, asked her about the incident, she said it never happened. I guess she preferred to be in the good graces of her older sister than being in the camp of her niece.

Two years before, I'd finally told my mom about the abuse. I wasn't really open about it. I'd just vaguely mentioned that he'd crossed the line with me a bit. But this time I bared my soul. I told my mom everything he used to do to me.

My mom was of course heartbroken for me when she heard the full story. I was very close to telling her what her youngest sister had done to me when I was a child, but the way she had reacted to hearing about her brother-in-law abusing me scared me, and I decided that she couldn't take any more of that unpleasantness, so I resisted the urge to speak.

Hearing all the details for the first time sent my mother into a downward spiral and into a deep depression. She was hurt to the core. What was even harder for her to deal with was how her sister had responded to the news of her husband's pedophilia. So, my mom withdrew from her younger sister and didn't speak to her for almost two-and-a-half years. She suffered quietly, internalizing the hurt. She lost weight. At one point, I thought she was even going to die.

Though she was living with me at the time, I didn't recognize that the loss of her relationship with her sister had been taking a toll on her. I was not sad that my mom and I were not speaking to her sisters, but my mom was devastated. I didn't need her sisters in my life. But my mom needed them. Her younger sister was her best friend, after all. So, you can imagine the hurt she was feeling.

My mom and her younger sister eventually reconciled, but I haven't spoken to that relative since our altercation. Funnily enough, having gotten that weight off my chest, I felt good. The past had caught up with me, and I'd had to unburden. I felt that if I didn't get the trauma that I had buried deep inside out of my mind, I couldn't fully become me. I wouldn't be healed. The brokenness I felt inside would stand in the way of my achieving any peace of mind and would continue to impact how I lived my life.

Because of the trauma I suffered at the hands of my relatives, I have trust issues. I thought the people closest to me needed to understand the reasons for my behavior in certain circumstances. So, I'd unburdened myself.

When I'd confided in my mother, though, it was a partial confidence that I'd shared, but I'd felt a bit lighter, like I had relieved myself of a load. When my mother's younger sister annoyed me and I'd revealed secrets about her man that she'd preferred not to hear and had blamed me for his predatory behavior, I'd washed my hands off of her, as the Jamaican saying goes. When she'd cursed me, instead of commiserating with me, she'd thrown back that weight of abuse on me that had been holding me down for most of my life. She'd made me feel like an outsider, someone who didn't deserve decency, or even her pity. She'd made me feel dirty, like something to be discarded. She'd broken my spirit again, the way it had been broken over and over again by people who don't wish me well. I hadn't expected that from her. Her reaction caused me to reevaluate our relationship, and I realized I didn't want to be in her space anymore, so I decided to walk away. I have had no regrets yet.

My mother's youngest sister made me angry when she denied knowing about the abuse, when on one occasion she'd actually been an eyewitness, if not to the abuse itself, but to the confrontation I'd had with my abuser. When she denied it, she'd showed that my feelings were not important to her. She, like my other abusers, had dismissed me as being good enough to be used for their purposes then discarded like garbage. I refuse to be discarded. So, I've told her and her sister what I think of their attitude toward me, and I've moved on. As I've said, I haven't had any regrets yet.

They may not think that I am much, or that I deserve their respect. That's perfectly okay. But I know that I deserve respect from myself. I wouldn't be giving myself that respect if I'd continued to socialize with these women, pretending that everything was fine. So, I've moved away from them emotionally and mentally.

My mother's sisters who I considered my aunts have died. The sisters who remain I consider her sisters, not my aunts. They have hurt me in ways that I am still processing, and it will take some time for me to forgive them.

Boys on the street

My abuse at the hands of relatives was just one of the incidences of abuse I endured. When I was in sixth form an incident occurred that still haunts me to this day. I had worn a baggy shirt to my Saturday class. I was on the Boulevard waiting for a taxi. One of the boys from Fulmar Drive walked up behind me and pulled the shirt I was wearing, causing it to balloon around me. I couldn't believe that he had done that. He'd wanted to see if I was hiding a pregnancy.

Such violation of my personal space!

So little respect for who I was that he was okay with pulling my shirt to expose something that should have been my business, even if it were true! This lack of respect is yet another scar that has stayed with me. How low must his opinion and expectation of me be for him to do that to me!

I cried that day.

I was living a nightmare in that community, and I hated it there. It was the place in which another incident of abuse would happen and would have a long-lasting impact on my life.

Rape

I was raped when I was fifteen years old by a boy whom I thought liked me. He was two years older than I. That boy and I usually took the school bus in the mornings. He would pay me a lot of attention, and I thought it was cool. We would laugh and talk about random things over the phone.

One day he asked me to help him with some schoolwork. I went to his house. I didn't want him to come to my crowded house in Ensom City. I didn't want him to see how I was living. I wasn't expecting anything bad to happen to me at his house. The boy was nice—tall and very handsome. Poor me! I thought that somebody that cute really wanted me to help him. But I should have known he was trouble. I know this is not rational, but he had a mole on his face, just like my mother's younger sister, who would later cause me pain. Probably that was a sign that not much good resided in him.

As soon as I stepped onto the veranda, he locked the grill behind us. I became uneasy and asked him to let me out. He refused. I tried to leave but couldn't. Two women were across the street standing at their gates. But how could they have known that I needed help? I certainly didn't scream. I did not ask for their help. Being the independent-minded person I was, I thought I could manage the situation.

How wrong I was!

Imagine my shame walking past them after the ordeal.

After he'd dragged me into his house and had his way with me, he went and bragged to the street that he'd bloodied me up. Apparently, I was one of the things to be checked off his hit list.

Imagine hearing that while still bleeding from the trauma he'd inflicted on my body.

After that incident, I came close to taking my own life. For years I prayed for harm to befall him, and I am not sure I regret doing that. He had a miserable end, becoming a paraplegic as a result of the way he'd chosen to live his life—one full of reckless abandon, I heard.

Recently, he died. His death didn't come soon enough for me. I just wanted to erase him and the memory of what he'd done to me. But the news did not do that, though. Instead of relief and closure, it brought into focus our past friendship and that awful day when he'd become a monster.

I've since given it some thought, and it has occurred to me that, like me at that time, he was just a child. He'd only been experimenting, and he'd chosen me to do his experiment with. I want him to rest in peace. He lived in a community where the boys in trying to be macho had done bad things to girls. That was the example he'd had, and he'd been playing out that example with me. I don't think he'd realized the level of pain that he'd caused me physically and emotionally. No human being could know that and go about business as usual.

His life had had its highs, and its lows, especially toward the end. He'd suffered enough. So, I will not dance on his grave. I just wished more parents would groom their boys to see girls as human beings with feelings and educate them about the psychological harm they do to girls when they choose to rape them for their pleasure. They can easily destroy a life, if the girl does not have the will power to bounce back, like I had.

All the abuse that I suffered took a toll on my confidence, naturally. I felt then that all this was happening because I had no father to protect me. My mom was forced to work extra hard to support me, so she couldn't have been there for me, which wouldn't have been the case if my father was present in my life.

The abuse from those boys shaped how I saw myself. I was beginning to think that my purpose on earth was to be someone's sex toy, to be treated with rank disregard. I struggled with these feelings in my early high school years. How could I have functioned optimally at school or in any other sphere of life with the memories of those events dogging me?

But there was much more abuse thrown at me, and it was coming not too far from home.

The neighbors

When I lived in Spanish Town, many of my neighbors did not care how they talked about me. They would be at their fence gossiping, and I would be in the kitchen doing my chores or whatever I was doing there, and I would hear them, saying bad things about me. I was confused. *Weren't they my friends?*

For me, Spanish Town was mostly a hellhole. Even though I had someone else building me up, the community kept breaking me down. Mothers of my friends would often speak ill of me to them and to other members of the community. I believe that they saw my obvious broken home as defining me and saw me as being repulsive and being bad company for their daughters.

As a teenager, I was naturally curvy. I had big breasts, and my butt was big, too. Those were some of the assets with which nature endowed me, things over which I had no control. I remember someone once telling me that I had the body of a slut. Can you imagine anyone saying that to a fourteen/fifteen-year-old girl going about her business? What do you think that observation would do to the psyche of that child?

That comment *huuurrrr!*

I understood it then: my neighbors *wanted* me to fail. They expected that I would fail and were celebrating the failure they thought resided in me, the failure they thought I was.

I began charting my path away from that community. I'd rather die than live there, I told myself. I realized that it didn't matter how smart, or how friendly, I was. My socioeconomic status was going to be that one variable they would use to define me. And they were going to treat me accordingly. I had to leave. It was sheer torture there. Anywhere was better than there, I told myself. To understand the trauma that resided in me when I lived in that Spanish Town community, not even on summer or Christmas breaks when I went home to visit would I ever stay there for more than one night.

Every time I think of Spanish Town, I smell the often-stagnant water from the blocked drains. Every time I hear the rattling of a grill, my mind is drawn back in time to the abuse I suffered from someone who should have been one of my protectors.

Spanish Town represented the hardest times in my life.

I was molested in Spanish town.

I was raped in Spanish Town.

I was talked about in Spanish Town.

I had friends who were not real in Spanish Town.

I was always being judged by my neighbors in Spanish Town, except for that outgoing Ardennite and that ultra-conservative girl who attended St. Hugh's High School who valued my friendship and I, theirs.

Things have changed now.

I've gotten successful, so I am feted.

I was born to a life of struggles, and I truly believe that without those struggles, as terrifying as they were, I wouldn't have been the tenacious go-getter that I am today. Neither would I have been the determined advocate for the voiceless in society that I am today.

CHAPTER 15
PROFESSIONAL LIFE

COCONUT RASPBERRY CAKE

Like this cake, my professional life has layers, levels and complexity to it. You have to be meticulous to get it right. I am succeeding at doing this.

Ingredients

¾ cup softened butter

¾ cup granulated sugar

3 large eggs, room temperature

1 ¼ cups all-purpose flour

1 tsp baking powder

1 1/4 cups desiccated coconut, divided

1 1/2 cups raspberries, fresh or frozen, divided

Extra raspberries for decoration (whatever number suits you)

½ cup seedless raspberry jam

Instructions

Preheat the oven to 350° F.

Completely line a two-pound bread pan with parchment paper. Put butter and sugar in a mixing bowl and beat until light and creamy.

In another bowl, mix together the dry ingredients (flour and baking powder).

Add eggs and the flour alternately to the creamed sugar and butter, folding in and mixing after each addition.

After mixing the flour and eggs into the creamed butter and sugar, gently fold in 1 cup desiccated coconut and 1 cup raspberries.

Transfer the cake batter to the prepared loaf tin. Level out the top and add 1/2 cup raspberries to the top of the batter.

Bake the cake for 1 hour.

If the top of the cake is browning too quickly cover cake loosely with foil.

Insert a toothpick or any other thin implement into cake. If it is relatively clean, the cake is baked. The cake should rise and spring back when touched and golden on top.

Remove from oven and cool for 15 minutes before removing it from the bread pan to cool completely.

Spread the raspberry jam on the top of the loaf cake, then sprinkle with the remaining 2 tbsp of desiccated coconut.

Decorate with extra raspberries.

I consider the starting point of my professional life to be after I graduated from Howard University. When I left Howard, I had a bachelor's degree in Clinical Laboratory Sciences. Having graduated summa cum laude, I didn't have much difficulty finding a job.

I started working with a prominent diagnostic center in Washington, DC. Because of my vast knowledge in the areas of Clinical Laboratory Science and having a Microbiology Specialty, I immediately began managing their department of Microbiology and Virology. This role allowed me to develop and hone my leadership abilities, as well as improve my research skills with the development of novel diagnostic tools.

I used the earnings from that job to take care of my mother, my student loans and myself when I was in graduate school. I even bought my first car, a used BMW 3 series, drop top (that didn't drop, but I was proud of it—hey, it was mine! My own dream car.)

My career was a bit unstable at that time, because my husband had just completed medical school when we got married and was about to begin a residency and a later fellowship, all outside of Washington, DC. This required constant traveling and moving from place to place—from the East coast to the Midwest.

It was during one of those moves that I became Vaccine Fellow. This work was primarily focused on vaccine development and efficacy. My lab at the time played a pivotal role in the research and development of an effective childhood vaccine. I was lucky to have joined that team, and I was successful in my tenure there.

It was while I was in this fellowship that I became interested in independent research and began writing grant proposals to conduct research in a field of my interest. One of the many proposals I wrote was of interest to a Fortune 500 pharmaceutical company. This proposal was to conduct vaccine research in the Caribbean. I was super excited that at my young age, I was Vaccine Principal, conducting research on my own terms, managing hundreds of thousands of dollars in grants.

My work then catapulted me to the heights of scientific research, and I was recognized and awarded the Junior Scientist of the Year award. This award opened so many doors in the field of vaccine research for me. I was invited to present my work all over the globe.

I presented my data to various congresses across South America and the Caribbean. Because of the vast knowledge that I displayed in the field of vaccines and infectious diseases, organizations and research and development firms began to request my input on novel diagnostic tools.

Soon after, I opened my consulting firm where I began working with biomedical companies on protocol development, standard operating procedure overview, and product development. After my children were born my firm began conducting more intentional work in biomedical advocacy. When I returned to school, The Milken School of Public Health, at The George Washington University, to study for a master's degree in Public Health (MPH). The focus of this work was in global health policy. Our firm currently supports the overextended public servants with specialized expertise by developing equitable frameworks and supporting various jurisdictions to quickly identify and determine key factors impacting the effective distribution of vaccines.

The most rewarding part of my career, to date, was being a vaccine scientist and being able to practice in my home country and the Caribbean at large. This work was supported by The University of the West Indies, Mona, Department of Microbiology, where I was a visiting faculty. I love the concept of developing and driving a plan for vaccine distribution and administration and helping to create robust centralized infrastructures that focus heavily on accountability mechanisms to coordinate immunization plans. My research has been published in reputable scientific journals such as *Nature*, *Virology*, *Retrovirology*, *Hemaologica*, *Blood*, *Plos*, *Investigative Ophthalmology*, *Visual Science*, *Read Eye* and *Contact Lens*.

All the work I do now must have a race equity and diversity focus. I am intentional about ensuring that what I do now, and going forward, benefits the poor and under-served while I continue to advocate for health and vaccine parity.

CHAPTER 16
MARRIAGE AND CHILDREN

CHOCOLATE CAKE WITH CHOCOLATE FROSTING

This is my children's favorite cake. I bake it for them all the time and it reminds me of family because we all come together to enjoy it.

Ingredients

2 cups sugar

2 cups water

2/3 cup canola oil

2 tbsp white vinegar

2 tsp vanilla extract

3 cups all-purpose flour

1/3 cup plus 1 tbsp baking cocoa, sifted

2 tsp baking soda

1 tsp salt

Frosting:

3 3/4 cups confectioners' sugar

1/3 cup baking cocoa

1 cup butter, softened

1 tsp vanilla extract

3 to 5 tbsp 2% milk

Instructions

Preheat oven to 350°F. Line bottoms of 2 greased 9-in. round baking pans with parchment paper; grease.

In a large bowl, beat sugar, water, oil, vinegar and vanilla until well blended. In another large bowl, whisk flour, sifted cocoa, baking soda and salt; gradually add to sugar mixture, beating until smooth.

Transfer batter to prepared pans. Bake until a toothpick inserted in center comes out clean, 30-35 minutes. Cool in pans 10 minutes before removing to wire racks; remove parchment. Cool completely.

For frosting, sift confectioners' sugar and cocoa together. In a large bowl, beat butter and vanilla until blended. Beat in confectioners' sugar mixture alternately with enough milk to reach desired consistency. Spread frosting between layers and over top and sides of cake.

In 2007, I told my friend, Allana, that I was going to meet my husband that year, before my birthday. We had a good laugh about that. Was I serious about that prophecy I'd made about the change in my marital status? I think I was.

I knew that I wanted to get married, but I didn't know when. When I made that prediction, it was because of something that I felt inside that I can't quite explain. I felt somehow the time was right for me to change my status.

Of course, my birthday came and went without even a glimpse of that husband. In fact, I spent the entire day in bed. Lanz, my friend who spent the day with me, gently reminded me about the prediction. That day she wanted to know how I expected to find a husband while I was locked away in my apartment lying in bed. I could always rely on Allana to hit me with reality.

As fate would have it, I got a new roommate, Kedz. She had finished her undergraduate degree and was about to start medical school on the 2nd of August, 2007, two months after my birthday. Kedz and an incoming freshman invited me to a rooftop party somewhere in DC, and I decided to go. Kedz, like me, is introverted. We both hated meeting new people, so I was her companion—her wing woman for that evening. Just in case.

The people at the party were loud and overly excited, but, surprisingly, with great personalities. There, Kedz found her voice and, well, forgot about her wing woman. She left me alone in a corner on the rooftop, where I met and began talking to the man who would eventually become my husband. He wasn't as rowdy as the other students. He was super friendly and had an awesome personality, keeping me engaged the entire evening. We talked all night; it was as if no one else was there.

Was I sure that he was going to be my husband? Probably not, but I knew that he was really nice, and I felt that he was special, because he was quite personable. We had a great time conversing and getting to know each other.

We both had our classes in the medical school, so we would see each other regularly. I was actually a Teaching Assistant in one of his classes—a Microbiology class, so I would see him in that class. We also met in the corridors because I would have to pass by the room in which he was studying to go into the Virology lab. Every time we met, we would talk.

I got along with his best friends (Brown Beads and Nuts Crew) and I enjoyed getting to know him. We were friends. We would go on dates and have a wonderful time. We were on the same page. He wanted to pursue me. I was ready to be pursued.

And then we became a couple.

Kedz would often say that she was the one who brought us together, but my husband's friend, Sola, would also claim that honor, because he was really our hype guy. He advocated for the relationship, and I am grateful to him for that. But really, I credit our meeting to Kedz, because she was the one who dragged me to that party when I wasn't particularly interested in going. But I also give some credit to Sola because he was the advocate.

Today, I'm married to a great, hardworking physician, one of the smartest, most respectful men on the planet—a real stand-up individual. He is loyal and trustworthy and family-oriented. Though he is a wonderful human being, the trauma that I've suffered has caused me to struggle to accept unconditional love from him, but he is patient and kind, and he gives me space when I need it. I know that he and my children love me very much, and I reciprocate.

We have two children, Kende, our son who was born in 2014, and K'nedy, our daughter who was born in 2016. I guess my family's penchant for creating names resides in me as well! Both my children attend a private Catholic elementary school. I know that every parent says that their children are smart. I say this with all modesty that my children are super smart. Whatever my mom saw in me when I was a child, I see in both of them. They are intelligent. They love school. My daughter reminds me of myself at her age. She is feisty—what my mom would call cheeky. Probably we're not so different after all, except that she is not afraid to stand up for herself. She is talented and enjoys dancing, swimming, playing the piano, and is on her way to receiving a black belt in taekwondo.

Dr. Foster and Family
Photo credit: Tunde McCrown

My son is also quite talented. At only eight he competes on the taekwondo circuit. He too is on his way to a receiving a black belt. He also plays the guitar, dances, swims and has taken an interest in Art which he does in private after school.

My husband is also a practitioner of taekwondo. He and my son have red belts in the sport and my daughter has a brown belt. I watched them practicing their moves and thought I could do it too. But probably I was thinking about preparing to defend myself if it became necessary for me to do again. Long after my children had started, I decided to learn. I've since gained a purple belt.

Sometimes when I was growing up, I felt that I believed in myself too much. It seems that I have instilled this belief in my children. My son will tell you that he is not just smart, but a prodigy. He has so much belief in himself, and I nurture his confidence. I see a little bit of me in him.

Sounds like they are doing a lot, right?

Do you notice anything here?

I give my children everything they ask for, including all extracurricular activities they ask to join.

Overcompensating? Maybe. I had a rough childhood in which I lacked many things and could not participate in all the activities that I'd wanted to. Since I can now afford to give my children the advantages I did not have, I will do that.

Like most parents, I want the best for my children, but I won't force them to make any career choices, one way or the other. Whatever profession they choose in life, I want them to be happy doing what they love. I want them to work hard for what they want, and I want them to be honest in their intentions, always.

I want them to be respectful and empathetic and I hope that they stay forever young.

I hope they stay grounded.

I hope they will find their own path.

I hope whoever they become in life will be a testament of our parenting.

And I hope they become individuals of whom they can be proud.

Our faith is a guiding force in our lives. I grew up in the Church of God of Prophecy, but now I'm Pentecostal, which is not surprising, considering the nature of both their services. My husband is Roman Catholic. That is one of our few minor differences.

My husband and I have similar philosophies about raising children. We place similar value on the role of God in our lives, and our children have bought into this philosophy. We also place value on family, on truth-telling and on kindness. I have been the beneficiary of kindness and goodness and mercy and that is how I've chosen to raise my children.

The glue that holds us together is practicing the 5 Cs of a relationship that his father always encourages us to do: commitment, communication, compromise, collaboration and cooperation. My husband and I live those five Cs. We walk in accord. Where I fail, he holds me up. Where he fails, I hold him up. We are a great team, and we have a great partnership and an amazing relationship.

This doesn't mean that we do not have our challenges. I am like my mom in some ways. I am not dependent on anybody for anything, and that sometimes put a real strain on the marriage, because I'm super-independent. I can get up and do whatever I want, because I've got me, and I can depend on me. If my husband decides to leave me—knock on wood that he doesn't! —I can provide for myself. I know how to provide for myself, something I learned from my mother.

I have multiple sources of income. The difference between my mother's income streams then and mine now is that mine are exponentially higher than hers when I was growing up. And, as my mother did when I was growing up, I'm always figuring out how to provide for myself.

My husband grew up with his family. He had a dad in the home, and he brings the good things he has learned from that relationship into our space. Our children and I appreciate that.

However, in raising my children, it isn't easy for me to give them all the space that they need to explore the world for themselves. My trauma still lingers. I don't allow my six-year-old daughter around anyone, unless she's at school, or I am nearby. I am so nervous to leave her in male or female company. I feel bad to be constantly watching these children around my child, but I can't help being nervous. I want to protect her. I want to prevent her from experiencing the horrors I experienced at her age.

I always wonder what I could have done to protect myself at seven years when I became someone's experiment. And, you know what, I can't think of anything. I'm aware that the trauma I suffered then is affecting how I currently raise my children. I understand that, but I think that it is necessary, as a parent, to be vigilant where your children are concerned. The most innocent-faced person in your child's life could have bad intentions where that child is concerned, and if given the chance, he can scar that child for life.

I know that. I have experienced that, and I don't wish that on my children or any child. So, I will continue to protect them as best as I can while giving them some room to explore their world, until they are old enough to decide what they want for themselves.

CHAPTER 17
BAKING

CHOCOLATE SOUFFLÉ

One feature of the soufflé is that it puffs up and is light and airy when it is baked. The chocolate added to a soufflé brings this dessert to another level with its smooth and decadent, rich dark chocolate and dark goodness. I have gone through the fire and I have come out like this dessert—light, desired, beautiful to look at...

Ingredients

1 tsp melted butter, or as needed

2 tbsp white sugar

2 ounces 70% dark chocolate, broken into pieces

1 tbsp butter

1 tbsp all-purpose flour

4 ½ tbsp cold milk

1 pinch salt

1 pinch cayenne pepper

1 large egg yolk

2 large egg whites

1 pinch cream of tartar

1 tbsp white sugar, divided

Instructions

Preheat the oven to 375°F (190°C). Line a rimmed baking sheet with parchment paper.

Brush the bottom and sides (right up to the rim) of two 5-ounce ramekins lightly with 1 tsp melted butter. Add 1 tbsp white sugar to each ramekin; rotate until sugar coats all surfaces, then tip to pour off extra sugar.

Pour 3 cups hot water into a pot set over low heat. Place chocolate pieces in a metal mixing bowl; place the bowl over the pot of water until chocolate melts; do not let the water simmer or boil.

Meanwhile, melt 1 tbsp butter in a skillet over medium heat. Whisk in flour until incorporated and mixture thickens, about 1 minute. Reduce heat to low. Whisk in cold milk until mixture becomes smooth and thickens, 2 to 3 minutes. Remove from the heat.

Transfer milk mixture to the bowl with melted chocolate. Add salt and cayenne pepper and mix until thoroughly combined. Add egg yolk and mix to combine. Leave the bowl above the hot (not simmering) water to keep chocolate warm while you whip the egg whites.

Whisk egg whites and cream of tartar in a mixing bowl until mixture begins to thicken; a drizzle from the whisk should stay on the surface for one second before disappearing into the mix.

Whisk in 1/3 of the sugar for 15 seconds. Repeat two more times to whisk in remaining sugar. Continue to whisk until mixture holds soft peaks and has a consistency of shaving cream, 3 to 5 minutes.

Transfer a little less than 1/2 of the egg white mixture to the chocolate mixture; mix until thoroughly incorporated, 1 to 2 minutes. Gently fold in remaining egg white mixture with a spatula until no white remains. Divide between the prepared ramekins and place on the lined baking sheet.

Bake in preheated oven until soufflés are puffed and have risen above the top of the rims, 12 to 15 minutes.

My astrological sign is Gemini: the twins. If we're to believe the horoscopes, there are two sides to the person who is born under that astrological sign, and that person displays both sides to the world. Having found baking and having been doing so well in that arena, while continuing to love and thrive in my scientific pursuits, I believe that I'm revealing my two sides. I believe that my introverted or private side is the one that engages with scientific things—my research and writings about science—while my extroverted side embraces baking.

I enjoyed the products that my relatives baked, but I never had much interest in cooking or baking—until 2015. That year, I had a difficult pregnancy. Bed rest was prescribed. That grounded me, which did not please me one bit. I'd had a demanding job, and I was involved in several other activities that I enjoyed. I like to be active. I like to be doing things. I like to be moving about. So, the doctor's prescription was a bitter dose of medicine for me to swallow.

After being miserable for days, I decided that I needed to do something before boredom drove me over the edge. During a conversation with my wedding photographer, he mentioned that his wife, who owned a dessert company, Mon Delice, was offering baking classes. I decided to take a class to break the monotony of being home, bedridden and having very little to do. I asked him to sign me up. I wanted to learn something new that challenged me, something completely out of my wheelhouse that would force me to focus. I didn't know that baking would be so easy.

Once I started, I realized that I had a knack for it. It was one of those gifts that I didn't know I possessed. It came naturally. Before long, I was baking my first cake. The first one was a two-tiered cake, which I decorated with flowers and butterflies. Everyone was excited about the work that I'd done on that cake. And since I was grounded, I decided to do a cookie class as well. That was fun! I baked cookies with a very good friend, Diwura. I wanted "Kate Spade"-themed cookies, so we made those. They were tasty. People liked them, but they were not my best. My cookie-making skills have improved greatly since those days.

Baking was supposed to help me to while away the time as I waited to deliver my second child. But it became so much more. After giving birth, I suffered postpartum depression. I became withdrawn, irritable and I cried incessantly. My emotions were erratic. The good thing about being in this depressive state was that I never once felt that I should hurt my child. Self-harm was the feeling I had to battle against, however. And I won that battle with baking.

Baking—a family tradition

In retrospect, my foray into baking is not surprising. I grew up in a family of cooks and bakers. My grandfather baked and I was often by his side watching him as he baked buns, bullas, duckanoo—Jamaican desserts. He also made bread, as well. He'd worked at a bakery for some time and probably learned the skill there or probably he took his skill to the bakery with him.

The maternal side of my family has a few bakers of its own, though. My auntie Nellie, my mother's late sister, was a baker. She baked fruitcakes and wedding cakes. She left this legacy with us in the recipes she's left behind.

A maternal cousin is also a professional baker and my mother, though not a professional baker like my Aunt Nellie was, can hold her own where baking is concerned. She provided me with invaluable assistance when I started out on this journey to bake and design cakes for my clients.

There must be a gene in our gene pool on the maternal side of the family that predisposes us to baking. Some of us activate it earlier than others. I activated mine quite late, and I am glad that I did.

Honoring my Auntie Nellie and baking her Jamaican Fruit Cake recipe on National Television. Filming an episode of Relish with Chef Yia Vang on TPT.
Photo credit: Chef Yia Vang

Baking: The early days

One thing about baking that inspired me to keep on going was how quickly I grasped the content. I was good at baking and didn't get tired of it. I could make six to ten cakes over three days and not feel tired or drained, because the end results rejuvenated me. Within three months of starting the class, I was making five-tiered cakes.

Six months in, I was mastering tall cakes, complex cakes and making deconstructed desserts. Deconstructed food involves separating the components of a dish and presenting them together. So, in baking, deconstructed desserts are desserts separated into their components. For example, typically a cheesecake is baked in an oven, and it has a crust, the cheese in the middle and a topping. Imagine the cheesecake broken apart and not in a pie form. It is now in a cup and not in its original container. So, we can serve the different components of cheesecake separately in a cup or on a plate. The diner chooses how he or she will consume it.

This trend of deconstructing desserts—to plate desserts in a nontraditional way—allows the baker to put a magical spin on any dessert which appeals to her creativity. This is one of the services that I offer my clients.

I can't say that the inspiration for the cakes that I create come from any specific stimulus. I just have a modern eye. I like nice things, so I like to create cakes with great aesthetics. I must have got my creative and artistic ability from my mom who is an artist in her own right, because she sews and has a good sense of style in everything she does, and my grandmother who is an excellent crafts woman. After I have created my masterpieces, I feel good. I feel a sense of accomplishment. I feel energized.

The first time I realized that I was good at baking was early in my baking career. *Elle Magazine Online* had reached out to me to ask my permission about possibly publishing one of my cakes. That was super early in my hobby years. I accepted their offer but because they'd reached out not long before submissions were closed, my submission was late, so I missed out on that offer. A day or two after I'd made my submission, I saw the published article celebrating the cakes that were submitted on time. I was really honored that such a magazine wanted to feature one of my cakes.

Who would have thought that someone who, for most of her life, had never had any interest in the kitchen would find joy in baking? I'd never baked a cake until 2015 when I started that class, and I'm enjoying it the more I learn about and practice this craft. Even though I'd been watching my relatives baking all my life, I find it difficult to understand why I got so good at it so quickly. I'm also struggling to understand fully my purpose in baking. Yes, I use it to mentor girls, but is there more to this hobby that I'm not seeing? Only time will tell.

My baking process

Once I close my laptop on a Friday afternoon, that's my signal to prepare for baking on the weekend. It will be an all-nighter for me until Saturday evening. I cannot bake during the week. Everything gets done between Thursday and Friday evening. I do not bake during the day. I respect my work time and I have to respect my direct reports. I have to be present on the job at all times. I do not cheat the system. I live with integrity, so I only bake at nights after I clock out of my job.

My administrative assistant sends me the list of cakes for the weekend by Wednesday, and I immediately start to think about the designs for those cakes. I flip through pages on *Google* and *Instagram* to see what's out there. But this research is not for me to imitate other people's work. My aim is to create original pieces. After I've come up with ideas for my cakes, I whip up my cake batter, bake the cakes, then chill them.

Fresh flowers are a big part of the aesthetics of my cakes. I chose to use fresh flowers not only because they add to the aesthetics, but also because of my baking schedule. I do not have time to make sugar flowers and dry them early enough to be put on my cakes, so fresh flowers are my décor of choice. But if someone wants sugar flowers, I'll order them from somewhere or make some. All this depends on the time constraints under which I'm working.

Sugarspoon Desserts

I own an internationally known premier cake and dessert business called Sugarspoon Desserts. When I suggested to some friends that I wanted to start a business, Dotun, the husband of my friend Diwura, who is a business owner in Washington, DC, encouraged me to find a name. I did and I chose Sugarspoon Desserts. My friend Nicole, the owner of Maggie Rose Events, and I brainstormed and came up with that name because we reasoned that we eat desserts with a spoon and the desserts are sweet like sugar. Dotun has continued to be one of my greatest supporters. He encouraged me to open my business, and when I moved to Minnesota, I decided to do just that.

I am well known and well respected because of my cake business. I'm a serial entrepreneur, so I have offshoots of the business—Cake Therapy is one. The other is a party rental company. I'm at a place in my baking career where I can choose my clients. My clients are the ones I've had since I started the business over two years ago. They love my style of baking, and they love my cakes. My aesthetic is very modern so, that's what I think caught their attention. I have a very neat, ultramodern style of making cakes, and I make tall cakes that appeal to the younger generation, since they like out-of-the-box trends.

I have a wide variety of cakes on my menu. I make multi-tiered cakes, double-barreled cakes—red velvet, carrot, almond, cookies and cream, raspberry, strawberry, lemon; whatever type of cake the clients need, I can bake it. Many of my clients find me through social media. Before I started baking, social media was in the background of my life. I have an *Instagram* page that I'd kept private. When I started getting recognition, I made it public. After I started my business three years ago, it became a place to showcase and memorialize my cakes.

Speaking things into being

It is said that we can speak things into being, and it seems that I've done exactly that. I remember when I was getting ready to defend my dissertation and was losing confidence, my favorite professor, said "You are great. You do not yet know how good you are. Probably you've been broken all your life that you are incapable of accepting it or even acknowledging it."

After hearing her say that, I paused and responded, "One day my name will be in lights." I didn't know how I would achieve that. At that moment, we both thought that I would have success through science, medicines and vaccines. But it was not this public aspect of my life that has gotten me recognition, but rather the private—my baking.

Baking has afforded me opportunities beyond my wildest dreams. With baking I've allowed myself to be seen. My cakes have allowed my name and my work to appear in national and international publications—on platforms many only dream of. My cakes have been featured in the *Black Business Journal*, *Perfete*, *US Weekly*, *Axios*, *People Magazine*, the *Jamaica Observer*, and on *ABC*, *PBS-TPT* and *Television Jamaica*. As I'm writing this book, the *Jamaica Observer* has awarded me their Food Award for having the most inspirational food story for 2022.

I've baked for recording artistes—both gospel and secular. I've baked for major conglomerates. I've also baked for major TV shows such as *The Bachelorette*. Importantly, I've baked for my two children who are my greatest supporters.

The Bachelorette 2021

The story of how I got *the Bachelorette* gig is a fascinating one. And it's pushed my baking career into the stratosphere. Sometime in early April 2021, Dianne, a friend, sent me a DM to tell me that I needed to check my email. I was curious, so I did. A woman named Brianna had emailed me and I noticed that she was a consultant for Warner Brothers, the filmmakers. Her email was not specific, so I wondered what Warner Brothers was doing in my email and what Dianne knew that I didn't.

Curiously I checked my *Instagram* and realized that there was a new Brianna following me. I excitedly replied to Brianna's email. In our subsequent communication she asked me if I knew about the *Bachelor/Bachelorette* series. I certainly did. It was one of my mom's favorite shows! When I shared the news with her, we were both in the kitchen. We were literally jumping around together in the kitchen. She began praying and saying, "God, this is more proof of the message you gave me when I was pregnant. I've always known, and you've continued to prove to me that your words are true."

Warner Brothers was filming Season 18 of *The Bachelorette* in Minnesota, and their 200th episode would be filmed during that season. They wanted a cake to celebrate that episode. Michelle Young, an African American who is from Minnesota, was the Bachelorette. They wanted a nice, tall cake. I knew I could make one, so I had no fear. I felt that the timing was right, and I was seizing the day. Their only brief was that they wanted the cake to be grand, it must have a *Bachelorette* logo charm and two hundred red roses. They left the design to me.

I rarely sketch designs before I bake, but I had to present my designs for Warner Brothers' approval. I called on my sketch artist, Tashane Bailey, a former UTech student like me, of *The Hand Studio* in Jamaica who'd done excellent work for me before. I explained my concept to him, and he went to work. Tashane and I went back and forth until we had four sketches for potential cakes I would make. We had all four sketched in black and white and four in color. Of the designs that I submitted, Warner Brothers chose the cake pictured below.

One of four sketches presented to Warner Bros.
Sketch Artist: Tashane Bailey (The Hand Studio)

I'd had a feeling they would have chosen that design because I had two hundred red roses cascading down seven tiers and in the center was a single-stem rose representing the final rose. Kudos to Tashane who helped me bring my ideas to life for that cake!

On the day of filming, I was given forty-five minutes to put the cake together once I reached the location. That time constraint was impossible for me to overcome if I did the job by myself, so I contacted my friend, Adam Gladue, a talented local florist who'd had national exposure from his appearance on *HBO's Full Bloom*. I asked him to take care of the flowers, which he arranged beautifully. Everything went well. I felt zero pressure. Maybe it was because I'd prayed about it, and I believed that it was my time to shine, plus I had my rider with me, my husband. Together Adam and I managed to meet the deadline.

I made two cakes for *The Bachelorette*, the seven-tiered cake and a two-tiered cake that was positioned across from the main cake.

On the day of the production, I turned up at The Marquette hotel where the filming would take place. By a strange coincidence, that was the hotel where I'd gotten married. In that moment I recognized the symbolism. I'd started a new life when I married my spouse way back in 2011, ten years before, a life that had brought me nothing but happiness. And now I was about to introduce a facet of that life to the world at the same place, and step into the public eye, something I'd shied away from doing all of my life. The Marquette was indeed a place of new beginnings for me.

I kept the news that I'd baked the cake for *The Bachelorette*'s 200th episode a secret for a long time. When the show announced its anniversary celebration, they tagged me on *Instagram*, and *Warner Brothers* had put out a press release that Sugarspoon Desserts had made the cake. Afterward that press release, my cakes started to appear in print and broadcast media.

The cake I made for Bachelorette, ABC 200th Episode celebration.
Flowers: Adam Gladue (The Full Bloom, HBO)
Phot Credit: Warner Bros

It was a special occasion, so the show's producers would have had every right to focus only on their celebration without mentioning my contribution. But they were intentional about talking about Sugarspoon Desserts. I was surprised. I was content on being known as Sugarspoon Desserts who'd made the cake, because I was still hiding. I was hiding behind that cake. I was hiding behind my cakes—the beautiful cakes that were my face, my heart—my everything.

Hardly anyone knew that I was the face behind Sugarspoon Desserts on Instagram. I was celebrating a birthday and posted a photo of myself. My friend Tanya Lee was one of the few people who knew I baked and that I was on social media, but she didn't know about my connection to Sugarspoon Desserts. When she saw my photo, she made the connection. She said, "Finally, you show your face!" From then on, we cheered each other on in our endeavors.

Jamaica celebrates me

When my cake was published in *People Magazine*, I jokingly said to her, "Tanya, call crowd!" This is a typical Jamaican expression when one is excited about something. Tanya took me at my word, and she did call a crowd. She brought my *People Magazine* write up to the attention of Novia McDonald-Whyte, Senior Associate Editor Lifestyle at the *Jamaica Observer*.

Novia reached out and expressed her interest in featuring me in the paper's Lifestyle section on Thursday, September 2, 2021. I humbly accepted. She titled the article: *A Jamaican Rose for a Bachelorette*, which I thought was really cute and crafty, and highlighted Novia's genius. I love the play on words.

She sent questions for me to answer. One of my responses was that "baking is what I do in my down time, after work, and it centers me." After reading that response, she asked me what I did full-time. I told her that I am a virologist and, more specifically, a vaccine scientist, that I did some philanthropic work, but baking was my hobby.

She kept on digging. I told her about my background. She seemed to have been astonished and intrigued that I was out there, and no one had heard about me. She wrote an entire story on the bits of my story that I'd shared with her which was published in *Style*

Observer under the caption **SPOTTED**. That caption was so apt. She indeed had spotted me. That moment brought me back to my conversation with Dr Paulette Ferbert-Harris, my favorite graduate school professor, whom I'd told that my name would someday be in lights after she'd given me that pep talk about my potential when I was about to defend my dissertation.

My entire Campion College class of 1995 celebrated me after they read my story. The ladies who grew up with me celebrated this win with me. I could no longer hide behind my cakes; Novia had outed me! I was complicit in it, though. I'd walked out willingly onto the platform that she'd given me. She'd asked me to trust her, and I'd trusted her with my story. She did a wonderful job at capturing the essence of my story that I'd shared with her. She's proved herself to be a trustworthy individual who uplifts women, looks out for their best interest, and celebrates them.

After my story was published in the *Jamaica Observer*, the next day I had an interview with Simone Clarke-Cooper on *Television Jamaica*. That article gave Simone a base to really ask me probing questions. I'd trusted Novia with substantial bits of my story, but Simone noticed the gaps and gently prodded me to fill them.

Family support

I have the support of most of my family in this venture, especially from my uncle Dockie, who is one of my greatest inspirations and motivators. They are amazed that I'm able to excel in this workspace, but I am not surprised. I have that zeal to take up challenges and to excel at them. Baking is one of the challenges that I have embraced; it's been good to me and I'm good at it.

Baking and advocacy

Baking has propelled me to advocacy. I use my cake business to host a non-profit called Cake Therapy. Cake Therapy is specific to systems-impacted girls to help them find themselves and regain their confidence, in the same way that baking has helped me. Many of the girls find this program after hearing about it and having an interest in what we offer. Others are referred to us.

I teach girls all I know about baking and have conversations about baking with them. I listen to their opinions and give mine, as well. I want them to learn to speak up, to say what's on their minds, something that I didn't learn to do for a long while.

I recognized my connections with these girls before I decided to work with them, because I could easily have been one of them. All the statistics said that I should have been one of them.

I was fatherless.

I was molested.

I was from a broken home.

I was in the doldrums of poverty.

I was rebellious at age sixteen.

I was in an abyss of despair when I was growing up. Had my mother given up on me, when I was going through my period of rebellion, I could have been one of these girls. I do understand girls who are in situations similar to what I'd endured, the ones who'd faced suffering. These girls have reacted negatively to the triggers in their unfortunate situations and were placed in the juvenile justice system.

They have been in foster care because their parents had no answers to what they were going through. These are the girls I'm targeting with my cake therapy. I've found that baking has allowed me to heal from a lot of the hurts that had plagued my life.

I also discovered that baking enhances communication. When I found baking and decided to create the cakes that I'd visualized, my mother was always with me in the kitchen. We talked about almost everything; the time we spent together in the kitchen was always one of bonding. And this bonding lightened the load on my shoulder and freed me to create. This is why my mother takes some credit for my achievements from baking because she was my assistant, my taster, my guide and my listening ear when I started baking.

My cake therapy really does help the girls who enter the program. Like any new program, some people approach it with skepticism and the pandemic has limited one-to-one interactions. The potential of the program to have far-reaching benefits for these girls is there, but it will take time. Those sessions that we've conducted to date have been welcomed by the girls who have reported that they've felt a sense of peace and less chaos in their lives after each session. The program is still in its infancy, of course, but as it is well subscribed and continues to help beneficiaries, and our work is publicized, others who need help are sure to find us.

I do one-on-one coaching with them. I teach them to make their dessert of choice. I take them shopping with me when I'm buying the ingredients. We make the desserts together. We take pictures of their creations and I encourage them to involve their children in baking as a bonding exercise. I bake with my own children, and I see how baking has strengthened my relationship with them. This is a gift that I want to give other parents and their children. I baked through the last three months of my pregnancy, and today my daughter has a keen interest in baking. I'm intentional about my children being in the kitchen. It gives me a chance to spend quality time with them and also teach them a new skill. I make all their birthday cakes, and they are usually pretty hands-on in making them. I experience all the good emotions that one does when my children and I bake together.

I am passionate about helping people, about contributing to the betterment of women and girls. I'm determined to change the trajectory of their lives for the better.

Reflections on Baking

My work in science has allowed me to travel extensively, and my work in baking has caused me to be featured across the world, with it appearing in publications in Australia, Nigeria, Europe and in North America and the Caribbean.

Baking, I've discovered, is my source of peace, my safe place. It is where I hide myself when I am most hurt. It relieves my anxiety and stress. When I recognized the value of baking and understood my reliance on it, I continued to explore online and other sources for new techniques and styles to try.

While I enjoy baking and I'm doing very well at it, sometimes I do feel like an impostor. I suffer from impostor syndrome because, while baking is only a hobby for me, it's someone else's livelihood. I'm privileged enough to have created my own niche in baking, and I protect my art form, but it is not what feeds me. I'm thankful for this talent, but it isn't my livelihood. My businesses are doing well—both my nine-to-five and my consulting firm, as well as Sugarspoon Desserts. This has afforded me comfort and stability, but it's time to get over this impostor syndrome. Baking is part of me now, and it is shaping my life in ways I'd never dreamed about.

I believe that my baking is a service and I always make sure that I'm using it in the best light possible. Even though I live in the USA, and I am grateful for all the opportunities and gifts the country has given me, I want to make sure that whatever I do is of service to Jamaicans and, by extension, Jamaica. When I started my business and I was recruiting workers, I ensured that they were mostly Jamaicans. My administrative assistant is a Jamaican who works virtually and the individuals who do any work for me are all graduates from UTech. I feel that I should keep this connection alive, since UTech provided the launching pad for me to jump off into my career in science.

Cake has been good to me. The more I bake the better I feel about myself. Cake has removed me from the shame of my past. It has allowed me to be more open to receiving compliments and staying humble. Once it brought me into the limelight, I couldn't run from myself anymore. My cake being featured on *The Bachelorette* has presented me to the world. My scars weren't on display, but the pristine parts of me were. When I realized that, I was able to see that I was the only one who was seeing myself as being unworthy; cake had allowed others to see the best of me.

Since *The Bachelorette*, I've done podcasts. I've baked on *TPT*, the local *PBS* station in Minnesota. I baked Auntie Nellie's fruitcake and made my grandpa's sorrel for the holiday.

Baking has also solidified my friendships. My friends were in front of me all the time, begging to get to know me, but I was keeping them at bay, hiding myself from them and hiding myself as well. Now I see them, and I'm sharing myself with them. Baking is breaking down that wall around which I'd enclosed myself and it is elevating me above my insecurities. It has shown me the best of me and is urging me to appreciate myself. It's forced me out of the shadows of who I once was and into the limelight where I can now look back at past hurts and shame and embrace them as the things that made me.

CHAPTER 18
REFLECTIONS

FRENCH MACARONS

I've had a complicated life, to be sure, and this is a complicated dessert to make. It has a hard shell on the outside when it's baked, but once cracked, the softest, most delicious filling is inside.

Ingredients

1 3/4 cups confectioners' sugar

1 cup almond flour

3 large egg whites, at room temperature

1/4 tsp cream of tartar

Pinch of salt

1/4 cup superfine sugar

2 to 3 drops gel food coloring

1/2 tsp vanilla, almond or mint extract

Assorted fillings (your choice)

Special equipment:

Oven with convection setting, 4 baking sheets, 3 silicone baking mats, fine-mesh sieve, pastry bag with 1/4-inch round tip

Instructions

Preheat the oven to 320° F. Line 3 baking sheets with silicone mats or parchment paper. Measure the confectioners' sugar and almond flour by spooning them into measuring cups and leveling with a knife. Transfer to a bowl and whisk to combine.

Sift the sugar-almond flour mixture, a little at a time, through a fine-mesh sieve into a large bowl, pressing with a rubber spatula to get as much as possible of the mixture to pass through. It will take a while. Save what's left in the sieve for another use.

Beat the egg whites, cream of tartar and salt with a mixer on medium speed until frothy. Increase the speed to medium-high; gradually add the superfine sugar and beat until stiff and shiny, about 5 more minutes.

Transfer the beaten egg whites to the bowl with the almond flour mixture. Fold in the egg whites.

Add the desired food coloring and extract. Continue folding until the batter is smooth and falls off the spatula in a thin flat ribbon; might take 2 to 3 minutes to get this consistency.

Transfer the batter to a pastry bag fitted with a 1/4-inch round tip. Holding the bag vertically and close to the baking sheet, pipe 1 1/4-inch circles (24 per sheet). Firmly tap the baking sheets twice against the counter to release any air bubbles.

Let the cookies sit at room temperature until the tops are no longer sticky to the touch, 15 minutes to 1 hour, depending on the humidity. Slip another baking sheet under the first batch (a double baking sheet protects the cookies from the heat).

Bake the first batch until the cookies are shiny and rise 1/8-inch to form a "foot," 12 to 14 minutes. Transfer to a rack to cool completely. Repeat, using a double sheet for each batch. Peel the cookies off the mats and sandwich with a thin layer of filling.

Harsh experiences

As I go through life, I regularly reflect on my journey so far. The low points of my life that were marked by harsh experiences and struggles and also the high points that are marked by a successful career, a happy family life, a fruitful hobby, friendships, the constancy of the love and support of my mother, relatives, mentors, and I've learned much about myself from these reflections. Not all the lessons I've learned about myself are flattering, but they serve as beacons, guiding me to a place of refreshing—a place in my life I eventually want to reach

The harsh experiences that I endured throughout much of my early life have shaped me into the person I am today. When I am annoyed, I tend to lash out. I do not engage in physical fights, but I've learned to fight with my words. I'm merciless in conflict.

Loyalty is a big deal to me. I expect true and unwavering loyalty from my friends, family, and relatives. At all costs. That's what I give. I'm loyal to a fault. I live my life with truth and integrity, and I expect that from those closest to me. Once this loyalty is breached, I'm tough and unforgiving. I'll cut people off without any regrets, without even a minute's thought, if they abuse my trust or hurt me in any way. Blame this on my upbringing, my lived experiences, which have hardened me and made me the person I am today.

I have been made a diamond from the pressures of my harsh experiences—beautiful to look at, desirable to many, desired by many but, like the diamond, I'm able to cut through much that needs to be cut. And life throws many things at me that need to be cut away before I can enjoy the peace and beauty that I need to make me whole. So, I will continue to cut away what needs to be discarded from my life.

I'm a product of the example that my mother's set for me. She was tough in every crisis; a no-nonsense woman who could cut through any obstacle in her way to get to where she wanted to. And she did that without evincing anger or any apparent negative emotion. She was focused on any goal that she set for herself and moved toward it with laser focus, prepared to move obstacles out of her way.

She was self-sacrificing, hardworking, and she was intentional about teaching me what success looked like. As a result, I had a map, of sorts, that showed me where and how to find that success. I followed her example, for the most part, and here I am today.

My family

I now have my own family. As I observe my children's happiness, and my husband's interactions with them and with me, I reflect on my childhood, and regret how much I'd missed. When I look at my own family, I'm in awe of what my husband and I have built: a community of trust where each member of the family can express an opinion and show an emotion, without being judged. My husband and I know that we are there for each other. My children know that we are there for them. We are comfortable in our relationship, knowing that storms will occasionally rage at it, but because we know that it is built on solid rock, we know that it will survive.

It saddens me that I didn't know how to trust at a young age, that I didn't know how to articulate my pain to my mom, because I now know that she would have listened to me and defended me with everything within her. I know this now because this is how I feel about my children, especially my daughter.

I know that I'm extremely loved by my husband and my children. I'm now beginning to accept and feel love. But the protections that I've had in place around my heart and myself are still there because fear continues to hold me hostage. I hope one day I'll be fully released from this fear. Until then, I will continue to make the best life possible for myself, my family, and my relatives, while remembering to share my talents with others who need a boost to get them out of the bad places in which they may find themselves.

My parents

I owe much to my mother. I owe her primarily for being a good example that I have chosen to emulate. My mom was a giver without expecting to receive anything in return. Her belief is that the more you give, the more you will receive. That belief has caused her to reap much from others, and from her children to whom she gave everything.

My mom has been the glue that has kept me whole throughout all of my experiences, good and bad. She chose to have me and accepted all of the challenges that life threw her. She wrestled with them and has overcome many challenges in her effort to give me that foundation on which to build our future.

My father was absent from my life until I was nineteen years old. His absence took a toll on me, but I worked through it, excelling throughout my school years, until poverty threatened to derail my efforts. "Teacha" was one of the nicknames that they gave my father. I guess that means he displayed some genius for them to give him that nickname, some genius which got derailed by certain decisions he made in his life. Maybe even poverty. If he were indeed smart, I have to thank him for the genes that he contributed towards making me. My academic prowess has been my meal ticket out of poverty, and it continues to serve me well, even as I search for other worlds to conquer.

I truly believe that I'm living the dream my mother had for me. I'm also living the dream that my mother had for herself. Instead of chasing her dreams, she chose to put them on the back burner where they remained simmering, while she paved the way for my success. She has molded me into the human I am today, and she can take most of the credit for my achievements to date.

She's also taught me the value of respect. She believes that if you respect others, they will respect you. From her, I've been learning to reject the "eye for an eye" philosophy. You don't have to retaliate because someone hurt you. Still, I'm also not the "turn the other cheek" person, either. I'm the "walk away from trouble" type of person right now. I won't be holier than thou and talk about not judging people. I try not to judge others, because I haven't walked in their shoes. I try to lead with kindness, doing good and taking care of people.

My mom said the reason she left Golden River was that she wanted the best for us, her children. She worked hard and things eventually worked out. Her children have now passed the worst and are doing well for themselves. She does not dwell on the struggles she went through to reach this point in her life where we have proved her predictions about us right. She chooses to focus on the end result.

My father, on the other hand, did the best for his own family, which I was not a part of for nineteen years; I never truly became a part of it. But I do thank him for the drive that his absence instilled in me—the drive to succeed, the drive to prove that I was worth something, the drive to lift myself out of the dirt, the drive to find myself.

He lived to witness a bit of my success, and I'm happy about that. I wanted him to know that in spite of his abandonment, I was still able to make something of myself. He saw that and was proud of what he saw. He was proud of me. He told me so, even though those words fell flat at the time because I wasn't ready to accept them then.

I need to let go of his abandonment, I know, which annoys me a little, every time I think about it. Probably, he'd done the best he could for me when he walked away from me with no intention of looking back. Probably, he'd thought that my mother was better suited to raise me than he was able to do at that time. Probably he saw me as a stumbling block to his ambitions, at that time. Only he knew why he chose to walk away. We never spoke about that aspect of our past.

But probably I should just bask in the fact that I got to know him before he left this life. Imagine the size of the hole that would have been in my heart if I hadn't got the chance to know the man who fathered me. I would have spent some of my life—probably not much—wondering what he looked like, wondering who my relatives were, wondering about that missing link in my life. I met him. The circle of my family life, although an imperfect circle, was made whole.

My Philosophy

I needed help to carve out a philosophy that would be a guiding light as I charted the course of my life. I got this help when I was in graduate school. I was working in the lab when an older woman came in. We started to talk, and she wasn't shy about talking about herself. She'd applied several times to enter medical school before she was finally accepted on her seventh attempt. She graduated from medical school when she was forty-seven. Some people would think that at forty-seven, a person shouldn't be just graduating from medical school, but instead should have been settled in their medical career. Typically, people coming out of medical school are between twenty-three and twenty-seven years old.

We got to talking about my next steps after completing the PhD. As we talked, she shared this saying with me: *Per ardua ad astra.* Which means "Through adversity to the stars." That saying, she said, had been her lifelong guiding principle. As such, she believed in herself, and she believed in her dreams. In spite of all the rejections she'd received when she'd tried to enter medical school, she didn't quit. She knew that she wanted to be a doctor, and she knew that she could be a good doctor. She also knew that it was only through attending medical school that she would be able to realize her dream. So, she persevered. And she reached the stars, the stars that she'd set out to reach, having graduated from medical school and being able to fulfill what she saw as her purpose in life—healing the sick.

She wrote those words on a piece of paper and gave it to me. For a long time, I carried around that bit of paper on which those four words were written, internalizing them.

I had suffered through many adversities in my life. These were the things that made my life bad—the poverty and the abuse. My life was a stream of adversities until I arrived at Howard University, which became my ark—the vessel that would lead me to a place of security and comfort away from the bad things that had surrounded me and threatened to overwhelm me. Once I reached the university, my life took on new meaning; my steps became lighter than they'd ever been; everything started to go up from then.

After completing my studies at Howard, I didn't know where the stars were. I didn't know what they even looked like. On reflection, maybe I'd already seen them but hadn't recognized them as such. I had two degrees, and I was working toward a third, so maybe those were my stars; at least some of them. But many more were about to present themselves to my gaze.

At that time, I was a successful individual by any criterion that could be used to judge success. Most people would have claimed their stars and would have been content, but that was not enough for me. When I started to kick down those doors that were impeding my continued progress, I felt my power, which caused me to paraphrase the titular line from the Helen Reddy song: *I am woman.* This line now reads: *I am woman and here I come; just watch me roar.*

Then I went on to break the glass ceilings that were preventing me from seeing all of my stars. After I'd seen them, I reached for them and continue to grab them as they get near to my grasp.

I was a young PhD. I got my PhD before I was thirty. Imagine that! After a life of struggle, wondering when my change would come, there I was, a young woman, making money and changing the way people did things. Having the kind of influence and impact that I was having, being just out of university was super amazing. I had passed through adversity, and I was among the stars.

Later, I decided to modify the saying to suit who I am—my personality and the way I choose to chase my dreams. So, the saying became: *Through adversity to the stars, with heels on*!

"With heels on" simply means that I can take on the world in five-inch heels, still be me and still be successful. I don't have to change who I am to be successful. I can climb the mountains and still be a girly girl.

This saying now reflects my life's philosophy. To reach where I am in life now, I wasn't afraid to be a girl. I wasn't shy to be a girl. I like fashion and I like to be feminine. I own that. I tell myself that I don't have to be masculine or adopt any masculine qualities or be as aggressive as a man to get results. I'm committed to doing me, and I've been doing that, and I've succeeded in all my initiatives in as feminine a way as possible.

I've made amazing progress on my journey thus far. But I'm not particularly surprised. I knew I had it me. I am smart. My mother had told me that, and I'd believed her. I put in the effort against the odds, and I succeeded.

I didn't do it alone. My village, Golden River, has some of my greatest supporters. But if, in 1983, you'd asked anybody in there who would be one of the success stories coming out of the community, I'm not sure my name would have been on that list. There were other contenders for this title—people who had money in my community. However, in terms of who would be one of the smartest children from the community, my name would have made that list. The people in the Golden River community believed in me when I was a little girl, and they still believe in me now.

The village that helped raise me extended from Golden River to Kingston and to the United States. In this village, people stepped forward to help me up the rungs of that ladder of success. For that, I will forever be grateful.

Coming to the USA was the change I needed. Here, I found possibilities. I found change. I found value. I found self-actualization. To have people valuing my contribution and to be able to value myself was one of the high points in my life. Even though I knew I had all that potential, I had some doubt as to whether I was valued or even valuable, because I was not treated as such by so many people.

Being at Howard, working hard, making good and being rewarded for my hard work in cash and kind, made me feel validated, made me feel that I was indeed worthy, as my first boyfriend had spent our time together showing me. I guess I wanted to hear the words, "You are valued," "You are worthy," "You add value to something" from other people and to be shown that by other people—people with clout, people who understood my talent, people who also believe that I could indeed achieve.

I've been on a physical, mental and emotional journey since I left the community in which I was born. Looking back on all the walking that we did while we lived in Golden River, I'm convinced that we were being strengthened to fight life, because there was a lot of fighting that we had to do to reach where we are today. I started this journey in search of more than I had, a journey in search of better. I found it and have been able to share it to so many people.

The road to my success was winding and filled with potholes. It oftentimes ran uphill, around perilous corners and down into dark valleys, but I've managed to maneuver along, and I've found my way out into a green pasture. I could not have done it alone, so I thank all the people who have helped me along the way for the helping hand that they extended to me. A number of guardian angels were instrumental in my success. Without them, my success might not have been guaranteed.

It took me a while, but I've found my voice, and I am not afraid to speak up now. I advocate for others and that's something I will continue to do. According to the prophet John in John 3 verse 27, "A person can receive only what is given them from heaven." This word is fitting to describe my achievements to date. If it were not for God's grace, I wouldn't have received any of the blessings that I've received so far. God has chosen to give me much. I'm mindful of that and will continue to give thanks by helping others who need help. My focus is on assisting girls who suffer from poverty, hopelessness, and abuse—the things I endured while I was their age—step into their purpose and make good of their life the way I've done mine.

I have stepped out from behind the wall behind which I have been hiding all of my life. I am ready to be seen, thanks to my cakes. But I won't be running soon. I have to feel my way through the blinding spotlight that is now on me and resist the urge to move back to my safe place—anonymity. I think I can do that, having now found my purpose after a long journey toward healing. I will get there just as long as I allow the good things in my life to embrace me, even while I return their embrace.

AFTERWORD

Forgiveness

Growing up, I often heard people say *I'll forgive, but I won't forget.* All the while the hurt they'd suffered was still evident in their voices.

I've thought about this phrase over the years and done some casual research on the word "forgiveness." I wanted to understand what the word really means. What I've gleaned from my research supports the saying about forgiving but not forgetting. Forgiveness means putting the hurt that one has suffered into perspective, with the aim of letting go of it. This is a process, and a process is not a one-time event. It's a series of actions taken over time to achieve something. In my case: healing.

The process of writing this book has been cathartic, but difficult. Dredging up all those painful memories hurt badly, and I found myself crying all day that first day when I started to arrange my thoughts. Of course, at the time, I did not link my tears to the subject matter with which I was contending. I wondered why I was so weepy, and then it hit me: I'd dug up all that pain I'd buried and so I was overwhelmed by it. The only way forward was to simply deal with it.

And that's exactly what I did.

I didn't change my mind about writing my story and retreat to that safe place behind the wall I'd set up around myself to keep out the bad things, to keep them separate from the rest of me. No, I faced them. As the memories reared their heads, I cried at the bad ones, and I laughed at the good ones. After writing down all of my memories, good and bad, and examining them, and after doing my research on the word forgiveness, I've decided that it is time for healing. It's time to let go of the hurts from the past. It's time to forgive.

Am I ready to let go of the bad things to which I've been clinging? In other words, am I ready to forgive? I'm ready, because I've been told that it is the only path to healing, and I want to be healed. This healing will change my life for the better, I think. It will make me a much better friend, a much better wife and mother, a much better person—who I want to be; someone who feels free to give the best of herself to her relationships.

In thinking about forgiveness, and starting to put it into practice, I am reminded of *The Lord's Prayer* in Matthew chapter 6, verses 5-15 and I realize that I haven't been practicing its tenets fully. Sometimes, we get so consumed in our hurts that we ignore the road to healing, although it's right in front of us. In this prayer, we're meant to ask God daily to forgive us of our sins as we forgive those who have sinned against us. But over the years forgiveness has been a one-way street for me. I've prayed, asked for forgiveness, yes, but it strikes me that I haven't extended forgiveness to those who have hurt me. This is something I've started to rectify now that I'm seeing clearly.

I've forgiven that boy who raped me. What he did to me was unconscionable, but I can see where his mindset developed. Taking a girl by force was the example that the adult males in the community had set for him. He'd followed that example, and I'd suffered as a result. I wish things had happened differently, of course I do, but they hadn't. I spent much of my life being angry at him. But it is time for me to let go. I've started, but it will be a process, and I acknowledge this.

I've forgiven my relative who'd abandoned me at Howard University. At least he'd left me in good hands. Everything eventually worked together for good. The university and Dr. Neita-Rosser came to my rescue by generously giving me the resources that I'd needed from him to start my studies. My relative is a good human being who'd made a huge mistake. I now understand his reason. If he'd shared it with me at the time, I would have been devastated, but I would have understood. From this incident, I've learned that communication is the key to averting misunderstandings that can lead to festering hurts. We've been communicating.

I've also taken steps in forgiving my younger aunt for the harsh words she'd tossed at me when I'd revealed my truth about her spouse. I've acknowledged that, just as her words had hurt me then, and still hurt me now, my words had also hurt her then and may even still be hurting her now. I was the aggressor in that conflict when I threw that stone at her, and she'd retaliated by throwing her own at me. I now realize that the way I'd blurted out my concealed pain was not the best way to have done that. But I understand why those words had escaped by mouth. After having endured so much for so long, one more conflict had been simply too much. It was the end of that road for me, and I'd put down that load. I now understand her response in the heat of the moment, and I'm actively working at forgiving her. Probably, it was her shock at hearing that her spouse was not as perfect as she'd thought that had caused her to be nasty. I'd had my reason. She must have had hers. I'm trying to let go.

Forgiving my mother's youngest sister is also a work in progress. There is much I do not understand about her. I need to understand her mindset, her motivation for doing the things that she does. Probably we need to sit down and talk, something that we have not really done in all the years I have known her. Probably, in talking with her, I'll find her saving grace, and she'll find mine. I'm willing to try.

The actions of my mother's sister's spouse still weigh heavily on me. Honestly, I'm not able to empathize with him. I don't know what could have caused him to think that what he'd done to me as a child was okay. I forgive him in the sense that I won't be dwelling on his actions anymore. But we won't ever be friends.

And, speaking of friends, I've also forgiven those who I thought were untrue, as well as the members of my community who made my life a living hell. They'd been taught certain values—what was good and bad, right and wrong—and I'd been taught mine. Unfortunately, these values did not intersect at that time. I'm sure that, over time, we've all been reflecting and improving ourselves and rethinking our attitudes.

For years, I'd held a grudge against my father. Even when I met him, and during the years that our intermittent relationship had developed, that grudge refused to go away. When he died the resentment was still there. But as I've thought about his legacy as it concerns me, I've realized that he had a big role to play in my success. Because he had abandoned me, I'd had this insatiable need to prove myself, to show others that I was worthy, to show others that I could be a success. If he hadn't abandoned me, I might not have been the success that I am today, and I might not have found myself. It was this realization that the resentment I'd had against him, that I'd been bottling up all these years, finally burst, like a dam overflowing its borders. Never to be retrieved again.

In writing this book, I've taken big strides, most of all, toward forgiving myself for spending all these years holding on to the resentments that I've nurtured after each trauma and forgiving all those persons who'd traumatized me. I've acknowledged my trauma and how it's impacted my life—not an easy task. It is now time to let them go. And I'm willing to do this. In making this assertion though, I'm reminded of the saying: "The heart is willing, but the flesh is weak." This is my state of mind at this time, and I know that memories of the bad times will flare up from time to time. But I also know that if I continue to hold on to my faith and grasp the good things in my life, I will complete the process of forgiving those who have wronged me. And hopefully, those whom I've also wronged will also extend a hand of forgiveness toward me.

ACKNOWLEDGMENTS

Writing a book is difficult, especially when it's the story of your life that's under the microscope. But thanks to the encouragement and understanding of family and friends, I persisted. I must thank my support team for being beacons lighting my path as I relived the darkest parts of my life.

First, I thank my mother and brother for being that unit that always provided me with refreshing whenever I needed it throughout my life. Without them being the constants in my life, I might not have survived my circumstances.

Thanks to my husband, Dr. Oladi Bentho, who has been accompanying me on this journey called life since we decided to be a couple. I thank him for continuing to hold my hand as I transition from my nightmare to a safe and healthy place. I also thank him for being patient with me until I was ready to tell my story and for being that steady, non-judgmental force in my life.

I thank my son Kende and daughter K'nedy for giving me the gift of being their mom and for daily showing me that my parenting has been a success so far. Their growth and development give me so much joy; joy that covers a multitude of bad things.

Thanks to my cousin Marlene who exemplifies the saying that "Blood is thicker than water." She's the closest person to me from my father's side of the family and has been a valuable friend since the day we discovered our connection.

Thanks to Tanya Lee-Perkins, Debbie Rhoden and Novia McDonald-Whyte who forced me into the light by encouraging me to take off the veil with which I was covering myself.

Thanks to Simone Clarke-Cooper of Television Jamaica for unwittingly planting the seed in my mind that the power of the pen would ultimately save me. This book is the germination of that seed.

Thanks to Kristoffe Lawrence, Janelle Waugh and Tashane Bailey, my friends from the University of Technology (UTech) whose commitment to Sugarspoon Desserts is unquestionable.

Thanks to the many guardian angels who showed up when I was at the lowest points in my life, from I was sixteen years old until now. Andrea and Trevor McLeod, Dr. Margaret Neita-Rosser and husband Dr. Rufus Rosser, Elizabeth Tolzmann, Tina Curry, Ray Moss, Zachary Hylton and Prince Corbett are among guardian angels who had my back every time the levee broke and the floodwaters rushed in. They took me on their vessels and kept me afloat until I reached safe harbor. I will be forever grateful to them for their generosity.

Since these guardian angels have helped me to reach solid ground, I promise to pay it forward by making my boat available to girls who find themselves in similar circumstances to that which I endured. I want to help them find their solid ground.

Finally, thanks to relatives especially my uncle Delroy, friends and well-wishers who are too numerous to mention here for their unwavering support over the years. I appreciate you.

Made in the USA
Monee, IL
15 May 2023